Creativ
Collaboration

by Nick Clements

First published in Great Britain by
Sound of the Heart Publishers, 2004

ISBN: 0-9547302-1-6

Sound of the Heart Publishers
Cilgraig
Capel Dewi
Llandysul
Ceredigion SA44 4PP
www.soundoftheheart.co.uk

Nick Clements

An internationally renown community artist who has worked with communities and creativity since 1975. He set up The Pioneers, an artist-led organisation, based in Cardiff, creating some of the largest public and community arts projects in Britain between 1981 and 2004. He has worked in over 300 schools, with tens of thousands of adults and children. In a variety of mediums, from paint through ceramics and mosaics to film and photography. He has taught and trained artists to work in communities in Wales, Britain, America, Germany and India.

These experiences have been drawn upon to create a series of three books which explore the uses of creativity and collaboration.

This book is the last in the series. They are for those who wish to use their creativity in communities. They give advice and encouragement to those seeking new and challenging ways of developing such work.

Other books in the series:

Pioneers Improving your school environment

The Pioneers murals,mosaics,madness and myths

Acknowledgements

This book owes a debt of gratitude to Steve Garrett for helping me with the ideas and concepts in the first part. To Maria Hayes who helped me with the second part, whose honesty in doing so was very useful, and who always inspires me. To my son, Tom, for helping me with the design for the cover.

Thanks to Sarah for her support over the past 15 or so years. I would like to acknowledge the work of the other 80 artists who took part in The Pioneers. I did not do this all on my own, I thank you for your wonderful skills, great ideas, help, assistance, bad tempers, tantrums, lessons and teachings.

Thank you for the faith shown by all the headteachers and teachers who let me make art with their children. Thank you to all the children who have taught me so much about myself, about the world and life. Thank you to all the institutions who let me work with them. Particularly to Jill Evans and the staff at Troedyrhiw Infants School who have been so supportive over many years.

I'd like to acknowledge my debt of gratitude to Ulli Becker, Brigitte Wachauer and Heiner Buschmann. You were never forgotten, but it was a beautiful surprise to see you all again in 2003. Thank you so much for being such inspirations to me. Thank you to Martina "Biene" Muller, I am in awe of you, and all the other children, who are now so grown up.

Thanks to those who have shown me the way, including Chris Elphick and Hazel Kirkham, Jack and Jan Angelo, Martîn Prechtel, Robert Light, Grandfather Wallace Black Elk, all my mentors. Thanks to Sid and Jules, the whole Rainbow tribe who have inspired me, and shown me how to shine. Thank you to Allan and Gwyneth who are such wonderful neighbours, as well as to their son, Owen, for his help in setting up the website.

This book is dedicated to my immediate family, Manda, Tom and Anna. You have inspired and grounded me through this journey, I am eternally grateful. Know that I love, honour and respect you, and really appreciate all the lessons you have taught me. Also, to the spirits and the land of Cilgraig in Capel Dewi, you have restored and re-vitalised me so often.

Author's Notes

These are confused times for the arts world. On the one hand there are major shifts and schisms arising- with rapid change and transformation clearly on the cards. On the other hand there are crumbling institutions. The stench of decay fills the air as outmoded funding patterns lie dead, but not yet buried. Yet, in this confusion, and time of fear, there is hope. A new breed of artist is emerging - one who cares, who works collaboratively and takes on social responsibilities. What do we call this new breed? - *A community artist?; an artist in the community?; a facilitator?; a community worker?; a therapist?* How do we define their work? What is it about?

I have been one this new breed of artists, and these are the questions I am seeking to address in this book. It is a personal response from an inevitably very limited perspective, but as such I hope it represents a step in the right direction. I wanted to look at how this 'community-based' approach to art has arisen – to uncover the historical context of community art. This publication is also a plea for community art to be taken seriously, and for artists to understand just how important creativity is.

The first part of the book, titled **"Creative Collaboration"**, is a theory which has evolved through my practice. It is specifically about the relationship between creativity and collaboration, as well as it's impact on society. The second part, **"Practical Creative Collaboration"**, is focused on how the ideas developed in the first can be practically implemented by individuals or groups. Before we go there however, I need to say that the views here are mine, the theory is mine. It comes after 27 years of working with people of all ages, and 23 years of running a community arts business. So, this is a very opinionated and personal view, I can write it in no other way. The community arts movement is crying out for a studied and academic history full of well researched and documented proof. This is not it!

I believe creativity is a fundamental human gift to our planet. We have a responsibility to share this blessing with each other, by doing so we share it with the planet as a whole. The beauty of our voices, the things we create with our imaginations, and our opposable thumbs, are truly awesome. No other animal has such gifts, and such a propensity to be creative. These talents and skills should not be hidden away or squandered. When we unleash these creative skills they transform and enhance the whole universe. Please consider that when you next put pen to paper, or draw breath to sing!

Many creative people are employed in a diverse variety of community settings. They use music, drama, visual arts, and performance - a huge variety of arts skills - to work with any number of different people. My questions to these artists are: *Do you actually know what you are doing? Do you really know the consequences of your actions, and are you clear about where you could potentially go with creativity and collaboration?* I believe that many artists are just skimming the surface of their own potential in terms of the effects they can have on society as a whole. Many creative people are just like me - groping and fumbling for new ways of working - and seeking new ways of ensuring their livelihoods. Central to this struggle is the search for proof of the validity of our practice, proof of the worth of creativity.

Intuitively, I and many other people, know that creativity can transform people's lives. However, we have yet to prove it. This book doesn't set out to prove anything. It tries to put into context activities which link creativity and social aims, and to give them a firm foundation. Conventional thinking about the arts tells us about the individuality of the artist, the separateness of creativity, the intellectualisation of creativity. I wish to challenge these views, and by telling another side of the story encourage more and more creative people to use their talents in a collaborative way. To change the world forever!

Since 1981 I have been called many things, in the beginning I was a 'student'. *"You must be doing this for free.....are you students?"* To expect artists to be paid to work with children was a bit much. When the question to one of my co-workers, was: *"Is he your father?"* I knew my number was up! Time to move on.

It has never been simple for people to comprehend what community artists do, and I have never been very good at explaining it to them. *"I'm a builder, I make mosaics with children, and I make art".* After many years of endeavour, I, at last, have some time for myself, and it is this which has enabled me to explain myself more fully and properly. In the beginning community art was seen as hippies painting children's faces, indeed most of us started off that way, but it has progressed and become very complex over the past 30 years. It is now a vast industry, hundreds of people are employed and tens of thousands of people participate every year in Britain, let alone Europe, and beyond.

For well over twenty years I have just done things. I have led a very active life, and the demand for community art is immense. It has left little time to think of doing anything else. Unfortunately, community art uses two of the most misunderstood words in the English language, both sadly mistrusted, so you have to believe me when I say such activity has been in demand. I think Su Braden sums up what I have been involved in, when she wrote in 1978 ***"The truth is that people make culture…it is active, not passive, it is neither a sub-culture nor an alternative. It is active and to be lived rather than passive and to be appreciated." *i***

My motivation for being involved in such activities is through not being good at anything other than football or art at school. When I realised becoming a footballer meant training really hard, abstaining from drugs and alcohol, getting up in the mornings……I went into the arts! I had a wide range of jobs for a number of years until I worked for three years in a Children's Home, where I discovered I could communicate well with children. I read and worked to the principles of A.S. Neill. I gained the buzz of being valued as well as being of value to others. Eventually, I studied film and performance at Cardiff Art College, and a small group of us collaborated and mutually supported each other through that time. Our work was funny, it was accessible, and deliberately avoided any intellectual interpretations. When we left College we formed "The Pioneers" and through a number of wild and exciting ventures we settled on working with children mainly in schools. Some of these stories are documented in the book **"The Pioneers - murals, mosaics, madness and myths"**.

We decided not to go our own separate ways as most graduates did at that time, but to form a group. We decided to continue mutually assisting and supporting each other. Most of the time there was four of us, but on occasions we had been ten, all of those working full time. The idea behind artists collaborating is not new. Artists have collaborated since the year dot - but it was frowned upon by the arts establishment - all the more reason for doing it! The collaborative process is complex, on occasions it worked perfectly, people intuitively knew what needed to be done. Individuals took on responsibilities because they knew they would be supported by the others. There was communication and a flow of information, ideas and energy. At those moments the product was always far greater than the sum of the individuals. To collaborate was to be responsible for your actions, but at the same time aware of how they are affecting others, this is borne of trust. On occasions the whole process ground to a halt. People became protectionist, trust broke down, arguments and strife resulted. At these times people left, others changed their approach, and eventually a balance was found again. However, this is an on-going process, it was never perfect.

As a collaborative artists group we were working directly with community groups, be they nursery schools, through to primary and secondary, special needs, adult groups, O.A.P.s, everyone. These people were gaining a huge amount from this process as well. I hope I will explain how that works during the course of the book, as it is complex and multi-layered. Suffice to say, for now, the act of making a work of art can be very involving - you need to be able to design, fund raise, get permission, make it, site it, maintain it. At the same time people are being confronted with their own self-values. The artists in terms of how they work, and how to share their expertise. The community participants in any number of ways - *'I can't draw, I can't make a mosaic, I can't do something that big'* - yet they achieve it, and then they have to re-assess who they are. Community art when it is really cooking enables people, hundreds of people, thousands of people, to make a positive impact on their own environments, their own worlds. That is a hugely transformative and powerful process, it can literally transform people's lives. They realise how good they are, how strong they are, how important they can be.

CONTENTS

Introduction

For over 27 years continuously, I have been combining my art with working in the community. This was not a deliberate plan - in many ways I fell into it. At school I only seemed to have an ability to draw and to play football (not at the same time). When I realised the levels of commitment needed to be a professional footballer, I decided that art might be a better option. But how do you become an artist? I was more interested in travelling, meeting people, and generally having a good time. After leaving school I spent a few years doing just that. Until 1979 I was sacked from every job I had. I drifted from being a road sweeper to working in Kentucky Fried Chicken, ending up working in a childrens' home in Hannover, Germany (that's another story). I eventually returned to Britain and decided to study art, which I did - firstly at Foundation level in Barnet, followed by Fine Art in Cardiff. This led me to a career as a community artist. Gaining employment for myself and over 80 other artists. It was a wild adventure from 1981 onwards and I made huge strides, mistakes, art works, friends, enemies, money, and losses before quitting my job in 2002, returning briefly at the end in 2004. That twenty-three year period forms the basis of this book. My experience and accumulated knowledge will hopefully be distilled into any wisdom contained here.

This book is not based on an academic understanding of creativity - it is purely pragmatic and practical. I want it to be seen as a principle that underpins a practice, not a dogma. The theory I propose stands as a challenge to establishment art theories. It is a small and deliberate attempt to question prejudices that have been given credance for some time. It is personal, biased, unbalanced, it comes from my heart, not my head. It is not backed by the present history of art, but I believe it is just as valid - indeed more valid - because it comes from personal experience.

The theory has to start with our creative past, but it also challenges the present, whilst attempting to clear a path for the future - a future in which we can all use our creativity in a collaborative manner. A future in which artists can re-claim their place as very significant players in civilization. I believe we need to focus on the benefits of creativity to society as a whole, and encourage everyone to act creatively and collaboratively. Creativity is seen to be elitist and specialised. As individuals we are all made to feel deficient, inadequate and unable to participate in creativity or aspects of it. *"I can't draw....she dances so well, I can't dance like that.....you've got such a good imagination, I'm just dull."* These are messages we have received from each other, from our contemporaries, and ourselves – messages that disable us and cut us off from our true selves. If we enable everyone to have access to creativity and let his or her creative juices flow, then society will change dramatically. The first thing which needs to happen in order to bring this about is for all creative and artistic people to start collaborating - amongst themselves, and with others. All other trades operate like this. A plumber can't exist without the carpenter, and a builder can't exist without the architect. Art has to grow up, stop being protectionist and small-minded, start being expansive and inclusive. That is where true power lies. Of course one book alone won't change this, but there are hundreds of community artists out there. Most of them want the same thing - to open out the arts and the way they are made for discussion and debate.

My real agenda is to bring creativity in from the sidelines, from being an insignificant part of our every day culture - something easily ridiculed. Creative Collaboration is a powerful message from an industry that has been sidelined and ignored. The work I do, and that of other community arts organizations and community artists, is not worthy of derision. It is not superficial, it actually serves a purpose, and it has changed people's lives. Community art has been about creating new communities. These may be communities that exist just for a day, or for a lifetime, but they impact on the individuals they contain. That has always been my aim. I have created communities, and by doing so have given the individual a sense of purpose. This is why I am trying to reclaim creativity's place in our present society. We have forgotten what it is to sit in a circle and share a story; to learn the words to a song together; to paint collaboratively; to decorate our clothing ourselves. We have forgotten how simple it is to be in community. And how simple it is to be creative. No wonder we haven't got a clue about how important creativity is, and the part it has played in the evolution of our species.

I believe that creativity can be a panacea for a great deal of the mess we have created in the Western European mind-set culture. If, as a culture, we were to have creativity as a core part of our civilization we would not be as 'poor' as we presently are. When we really encourage children to use their creativity throughout school rather than repressing it, we will have a very different education system. We have reaped the consequences of ignoring creativity, marginalising it, and creating a 'scientific' and 'mind' orientated culture. Creativity stems from the imagination, the unconscious, and we need to access that more and more. Creativity is a life function like eating, breathing and procreation. Creativity creates culture because it is inextricably linked to intelligent behaviour. As individuals we adapt, we recognize our surroundings and make things happen. We create solutions - it is a fundamental cornerstone of our humanness. The application of creativity, the use of imagination by mature and responsible human beings, can create social change on a massive scale. There is now a multi-million pound industry employing artists to work collaboratively in community settings. This is a real growth industry that has only come to the fore in the past 20 years. It is a very strong and positive alternative to what can be for many people the alienating 'high art' of opera, galleries and museums.

In order for this book to serve its purpose I will begin with where community art comes from. I started to write this about two years ago. At that time I saw the roots of such activities as being in the 1960's. As I have developed my theoretical perspective I realized that I needed to go further back. The roots of community art are pre-historic. To simplify matters I have looked at it through the development of two strands, namely 'creativity' and 'collaboration'. These are two separate yet linked strands of human evolution. In my view they are the most important factors in the advancement of any civilization, and are essential to the creation of a culture. To prove that, I will delve back and grasp the essence of our cultural heritage. To offer an updated understanding of who we are, and where we all come from.

The second part of the book is a more practical guide to such activities, how to apply them, how to mutually support, and how to create more in the future.

Creative Collaboration

Chapter One

The role of creativity in the evolution of human beings

Science hasn't helped us to evolve as a species. As an artist, that feels good to say. Scientists are always telling anyone who'll listen how important their subject is. Yet in historical terms it is a very recent phenomena, with no relevance to our evolution. I believe you have to be creative to understand science, but understanding science gives you no understanding of creativity. Our creative urges were the key to our evolution over the past millennia, and our innate creativity has enabled us to behave in an intelligent way. As science evolves it only helps us understand quite how important art and creativity are. Great advances in science only came through the application of creativity. Newton, Einstein, Darwin - they all did the same thing. They stepped beyond the bounds of the established order, they thought outside the existing framework. That's what artists do all day! Creativity is a gift which we all carry. It is actually a survival tool for humanity, and without it we would die. Art and creativity are ancient practices, they are one of the earliest things we did as humans.

If we agree that creativity is a basic human instinct, we can understand that humans have been creative since the beginning of time. The need for self-expression can be seen in cave paintings; in ornate carvings on tools; and in decorative finishes on clothing. Humans have also made highly creative use of their voices. All societies had songs and stories which were an integral part of their culture - knowing who they were. Humans have a huge tradition of dance and music. We have sung; told stories; made music; danced and decorated since the beginning of time. These activities have had the initial effect of making people happy.

This may seem superficial, but it is very important, as it provides the social 'glue' that binds a group of individuals together. From the earliest days it was important for humans to work in teams. Hunting and gathering are not solitary tasks. Creativity generated tangible and easily recognizable signs of belonging. By knowing how to decorate yourself and your clothing, you showed your identity. By learning your tribes' songs and stories you showed where you belonged. By participating in your dances and music you bonded with your peers. Creativity was highly important in those early days. Everyone needed to be able to participate in all areas of creative activity, and this attitude to 'the arts' remains with what we arrogantly describe as 'primitive' peoples today. Everyone sings along; knows the words; knows the patterns; knows the meanings; knows their part in society through their creativity. Many of these early cultures have no word for 'art' - there is no separation - no 'artist' - there just is culture as the ubiquitous backdrop to everything.

I believe this is how far back community art really goes. This shows how significant creativity is. It created society. The very fabric of civilization has been, and continues to be woven by creativity- not science, not physics, not mathematics, not algebra. We have filled our society and culture with other disciplines, and have made them more important than creativity. We have turned our back on our own true nature. Art historians have collaborated in this whole process by not challenging the status quo.

"..art, however one defines it, must still mirror, favourably or with hostility, the development of the society to which it belongs." *ii This is true, but it ignores the fundamental truth that creativity made society in the first place!

Modern anthropology, as it develops and becomes more creative, is starting to understand the complexity of our past. Human beings have not been living in little settlements and ignoring each other for millions of years. The stereotypical view of cavemen huddling separately in their caves is wrong. They were creative, imaginative, and had large workshops in which were manufactured goods, fabrics and decorative works.

The Lakota Sioux, one of the great Native American Indian tribes, were nomadic. They traveled from Canada to Mexico, the length of North America each year. Not because they were hungry and driven by deprivation, but because they chose to follow the sun. They remained in the North during July and in the South during December. Because of this movement they had contact with other tribes with which they traded. They were incredibly sociable, well traveled and intelligent. Through this trade they shared their arts and crafts, they learnt other skills and they created new ones. Medieval rural settlements in Britain were not intransigent and in-bred. The peasants 'drove' their cattle, sheep and pigs hundreds of miles every year. West Walian communities traded their animals in London - a feat we would find impossible to achieve nowadays. People have always been by nature very flexible. Communities have a tendency towards outward looking, and humans have always sought to travel and grow in intelligence.

We need to see that our past, both distant and recent is not as we have been taught at school and through the media. We are intelligent and creative people, and as such we are no different from those first 'cave men'. They were also intelligent and gregarious people who used their imaginations and creativity to sustain themselves. We have not evolved in any aspect of physiology for many hundreds of thousands of years.

** I believe when we use our creativity we increase our intelligence.*

When we are set a problem we need to use our creativity to solve it, and then we pass the information on, creative collaboration in action.

** We extend our life expectancy by forming communities and by passing on information.*

When we apply creativity and we collaborate with others we live longer, we are healthier, we advance as a race. This was the approach used by the most successful and enduring societies in the past, and it will be used by them in the future. This process occurs through the stories, the songs, the dance, the music and the drawings which collectively makes up the 'culture' of a society. This was how civilization was spread, and will be in the future.

This has been recognized within most anthropological works. Scientists don't use the same terms as I do to describe it, but to quote Jared Diamond.

"Group cohesion depends on the group's distinctive culture – especially its language, religion, and art (including stories and dances), hence art is a significant force behind group survival." *iii

So, creativity has been the driving force behind the evolution of mankind. We increased our intelligence through the application of creativity, and we lived longer. This is often overlooked in modern education, I certainly was never taught this. In addition, schools now evaluate our children's intelligence in terms of science, mathematics, reading and writing. However if we are actively stimulating our creativity and using our imaginations we are showing greater signs of learning, understanding and adapting. To repeat facts and dates 'parrot fashion' is neither creative nor intelligent. To use our creativity is to be able to find the solutions that are not immediately visible, or probably in the text book, is the way forward.

I believe being creative is not enough. We need to be able to use creativity for the good of others as well. When we liberate ourselves in this way we can be creative in any way we choose. It could be in painting, dancing, singing, making music, decorating, story telling. These are the most common and familiar forms of creativity. But, importantly, we need to start seeing that creativity is not tied to just these few activities. Creativity is a way of being, a way of living, and a way of relating to others. We can apply the principles of creativity throughout all aspects of our lives in order to create social improvement. The community development work I am presently involved in - the creation of jobs, sustainable energy schemes, and reminiscence projects - are a direct result of applied creativity. When people are confident of their ability to see the solutions to small problems, they can venture into a very wide range of responses and larger problems. I believe that by applying creativity to all aspects of our lives we will bring about radical social change. Applied creativity comes from a position of strength from which vision and compassion can be applied to community problems. The application of creativity happens all the time, all around us – it's just that we don't recognize it as such. The culture in which we live likes to compartmentalize everything, and by doing so, it restricts our understanding and our ability to see the 'bigger picture'. The 'bigger picture' is that artists, dancers, musicians are a potent force for social change. The problem is that most of *them* don't recognize it within themselves, let alone know how to fulfil such a potential.

Chapter Two

Collaboration as a means of advancement

Collaboration is the other foundation stone of human civilization and evolution. In order to fully appreciate the significance of collaboration in terms of evolutionary advancement we need to be able to understand Darwin's view, as well as some of his contemporaries, particularly Wallace and Kropotkin. This may seem a little complex for a book about art, but I believe it is very important in terms of our understanding of why collaboration needs to be linked to creativity. The premise of Darwinism, and Wallace's interpretation of it, is quite simple. By recognized the different species and categorizing them, they recognised common traits. They noticed that each species tried to ensure it's longevity by procreating and bringing up the next generation. As they examined this simple premise they came across an interesting characteristic – the individuals all tended to form into 'families' or groups. This seemed to enhance their survival potential, and specifically their ability to survive the following threats.

* *The forces of nature – weather, climate, geography, topography, etc,.* This is the most powerful force in the process of natural selection, it is by far the largest factor in determining the survival of individuals and species.
* *Natural predators* –larger animals or smaller pests; by viruses and bugs; by invasive plants even.
* *Other species competing for their habitat, food, etc.* A relatively small but still significant factor.
* *Fellow members of the species especially at mating time, etc.* In comparison to the other factors this is a minimal risk.

Adapted from Darwin

The threats to all species were in this order to reflect their relative importance. The first factor creates the greatest threat to individuals, the last the least. This is worth noting, because as humans in our individualistic culture we have focused on the last factor, believing it to be the most important, mainly because it is about the individual. This is not the case. The weather causes far more damage to all species, including humans, and the interaction between individuals is relatively unimportant.

Through spending time in 'virgin' jungles, forests and landscapes the early anthropologists were able to observe nature before 'civilized man' interfered. They were struck by the diversity of species; the sheer numbers of individuals; the cohesive nature of such environments; and the collaboration between the species they observed. From their observations they came to the idea of natural selection as a response to all the above threats, which were assumed to be constantly present. These threats were seen to affect all of the individuals within the species. Those individuals able to adapt in ways which enabled them to resist or cope with those threats survived. It was seen as being that simple.

The process of adapting to survive, or failing to adapt and dying out, was assumed to have been going on for millions of years. The species which were well adapted to their environment continued - those that weren't fell by the evolutionary wayside. It seemed to be a clear-cut conclusion, and as they looked at the application of this formula they saw how it certainly applied throughout the natural world. They then looked at how this simple process was avoided or 'cheated' by certain species and individuals. As they looked they kept coming back to the fact that those who formed groups stood a better chance of surviving. In every natural circumstance, the herd, the shoal, the flock, and the pack were shown to be far superior to the lone individual in terms of survival. Natural selection therefore predicted that those individuals forming groups stood a better chance of surviving. Darwin was happy with that, and Wallace agreed. Kropotkin, however, saw this as being just the first stage of a process. He believed that it was not just the individuals who formed groups which enabled their species to survive, rather it was the individuals who formed support structures within their groups, and then mutually supported *other species* which survived. This is not taught in the textbooks on Darwinian theory, this is the element that I believe we need to concentrate on. In summary - *Those species, which mutually support other species, will survive; those that act from individual greed will become extinct.*

To expand this proposition a bit further, we need to understand the role of the individual in a society. Any individual from a species has two ways of behaving - either forming groups or making provisions only for themselves. These are not equally effective survival strategies. The first is by far the most successful. The group urge protects individuals in the short and long term. The individual urge ensures progress and reduces inertia in the short term, and encourages innovation. We can call the two forces which every individual and species has within them 'mutual aid' and 'individualism'. Our whole culture has become so enthralled by 'individualism' we have created a different understanding of the word.

"I should certainly be the last to underrate the part which the self-assertion of the individual has played in the evolution of mankind. However, this subject requires, I believe, a much deeper treatment than the one it has hitherto received. In the history of mankind, individual self-assertion has often been, and continually is, something quite different from, and far larger and deeper than, the petty, unintelligent narrow-mindedness, which, with a large class of writers, goes for "individualism" and "self-assertion."*iv

Our short-term understanding and cultural prejudice cloud our understanding of 'individualism'. We need to see the deeper and more important role it plays within evolution. I believe this is tied to the assertiveness, the commitment to progress and the un-impeachability of loving and caring behaviour. Altruism is the natural state of humans. We have used a very perverse interpretation of individualism to create a very unnatural culture where we feel ourselves to be beyond the forces of natural selection. We have lost touch with the principle of, and instinct for, collaboration.

"In the animal world we have seen that the vast majority of species live in societies, and that they find in association the best arms for the struggle for life: understood, of course, in its wide Darwinian sense – not as a struggle for the sheer means of existence, but as a struggle against all natural conditions unfavorable to the species. The animal species, in which individual struggle has been reduced to its narrowest limits, and the practice of mutual aid has attained the greatest development, are invariably the most numerous, the most prosperous, and the most open to further progress. The mutual protection which is obtained in this case, the possibility of attaining old age and of accumulating experience, the higher intellectual development, and the further growth of social habits, secure the maintenance of species, its extension, and its further progressive evolution. The unsociable species, on the contrary, are doomed to decay."*v

It seems, then, collaboration is the key to our survival, and collaboration on a global scale with other species will ensure our species' survival, as well as all the other species.

Chapter Three
The artists' role in society

The previous chapters outlined the importance of creative collaboration, and indicated how its application can improve society and effectively serve to create what we refer to as 'culture'. To develop this proposal further we need to see what the historical role of the creative person has been in society. Creativity has been able to hold society together and to move it on. Creative individuals did this by using two forms:-

- *their individual practice*
- *the shared community experience*

* *Individual practice*

This was undertaken in the true sense of 'individualism" - for the advancement and betterment of society. For the sake of my argument I make no distinction between artist and craftsperson, I know many people do, but there is a close connection. Artists, craftspeople and artesans were not separated for many thousands of years. For the sake of clarity, I'll call them all artists. These people were recognised as being gifted and having something of value for society. Artists had a function as members of the community as did those who plied every trade within it. Individually they had talents in certain areas such as singing, music, painting, dancing, making, etc. Their responsibility was to develop these skills. Once an individual was identified as having skills or a leaning towards a certain area, they were trained in the discipline and apprenticed to a range of masters in order to learn all there was to know about that 'trade'. This process could take quite some time.

The artists needed to know the culturally accepted history of their chosen trade. Once they were engaged in this form of training they could start to experiment with the materials. As their knowledge and expertise grew their experimentation could become more advanced. At the conclusion of their apprenticeship they could become accepted as a master/mistress. The whole system was geared to encourage each generation to go beyond their teachers and extend their skill into new and undiscovered areas.

Once they had become a master/mistress they would ply their trade and earn a living through their skills. As part of this process their responsibilities were also to extend the knowledge about the tools and materials they used into new areas, creating new ways of doing things and artistic innovations. These new ways of working would gradually be absorbed into the trade as a whole. This could only take place if each generation took apprentices and passed their innovations on. As individuals were extending their existing trade, they would pass on the historical context and knowledge of their art or craft, as well as their newly developed interpretations. This model of artistic evolution existed for thousands of years. However, it broke down hundreds of years ago. Since then new innovations have been kept as individual skills which can die with the individual, and at the same time the 'historical knowledge' has been lost, so trades come and go.

One example of this flux, from the many I could choose, is the harp making industry of Wales and Britain. Living in West Wales I presumed that there had always been a harp making industry there, but it is only when I explored the history of such a craft that I saw how tenuous and thin the connections are to the past. The harp industry's heyday was between 1811 to 1850, due to the development of the harp as a chromatic instrument as opposed to the folk based diatonic models of before. This development was down to one man: Erard, of France, who created the modern day version of the ‘withdrawing room instrument’ that we all know and love. But the mass production of the piano from 1850 onwards meant the demand for harps dwindled. The Russian revolution meant the end of Erardes in 1917. From that point onwards, there were no new harps being created, only old ones being repaired. Not until the 1960’s with Salvi in Italy, linking to the decline in the Swiss clock making industry which freed up a large number of very skilled workers, were any new harps made. After making a set of miniature tools and a miniature orchestra in the early 1950’s John Thomas of Cardiff, a fourth generation carpenter, started to work on making full-scale harps in Wales. Fascinated by the miniature harp he had made for a commission, he attempted to create actual working models, and by the early 1960’s was selling and making Celtic and Triple harps. It was not until Allan Shiers and other apprentices had been taken on by John Thomas, and the development of a School of Musical Instrument Making in Abertridwr, that finally in 1986 the first concert quality harp was made in Wales. The harp-making tradition in Wales is still hugely endangered as Allan and others strive to build a small community business in West Wales to preserve the skills and techniques they have learnt. It is amazing how these skills vanish and then appear again. For 50 years no new harps were made in Wales, and it took about 20 years to re-learn and develop these skills.

* *Shared community experience*

The second part of the artist’s former role in society is more difficult to trace, as it disappeared a longer time ago. It entails the retention and passing on of the shared ‘community use’ for a particular trade. This is the ‘mutual aid’ part of an artists’ responsibilities. This element was not only particular to a trade, but also linked into the community as a whole. In music it was the tunes which accompanied certain ceremonies or rituals. In decoration it was the story behind the patterns. Artists needed to be aware of the cultural significance of their trade, and they were taught this as part of their apprenticeship. So, in spite of being individual specialists in a trade, they shared in and contributed to, the community experience. They held the community together through being able to create the songs, music, arts and crafts which were essential in certain ceremonies or rituals at important times of year. These told the community where they came from, 'their origin stories', and created a cultural context for community life. Artists had the skills which were needed at particular times - harvest time, winter solstice, etc. – and they created the space in which renewal and remembrance occurred. This process was linked to the spiritual well being of their culture, and underpinned the survival of their village or community.

In a sense the artist's role was to maintain the status quo. Being an artist or a craftsperson was an important part of society and they were significant players in the cultural heritage and development of the civilization. We have been denied this truth in the past few hundred years and we have suffered as a culture, and as a world as a consequence. For me this leading role for art and creativity in the advancement of society helps explain another very important element of our appreciation of creative collaboration. When rituals and ceremonies are being undertaken in indigenous cultures they are seen as 'healing', or as a 'remembrance' of how things should be. Most societies are so busy in their pursuit of 'individualism' they need a ritual or ceremony every now and again to bring its members back into equilibrium. Artists, together with the shaman, the elders and others, can bring society back into balance. I believe this is a very significance part of the artist's role. When we work with creativity and we work in a collaborative fashion, we can actually be a healing influence on individuals and society as a whole. Throughout history artists were involved in healing - maybe not as directly as the shaman or other doctors, but they were part of the overall picture of health for a given society. Indeed our ancestors knew all about the therapeutic healing and recuperative powers of creativity. Creativity was always used as a means of healing peoples' lives and as a means of developing people's identity and cohesion. It was seen as a powerful tool, and the artist was well respected, honoured by the community as a whole. We're only just rediscovering this truth after many hundreds of years of denial.

This was the complete picture of the artist. They advanced their own trade through individual endeavour, and then through the sharing of knowledge they ensured cohesion and balance within their communities. Through their teaching, and by creating and contributing to ritual and ceremony they also ensured the well-being of society. We have lost contact with and knowledge of these functions. Today's artists are taught that they are first and foremost individuals. They are encouraged not to pass on particular skills or any advancements they may have made. They do not hold their society together through their trade.

The model of apprenticeship which taught artists and craftspeople about the cultural significance of their trade and their history is centuries old, possibly hundreds of thousands of years old. As we have become more 'civilized' we have lost these layers of meaning and significance - our ancient histories, our past. Christianity had a major role in eroding the 'ceremonial' and 'mystical' significance of certain music, dance, decorations and other arts. Once this deeper level of meaning was lost apprentices were only being taught the superficial skills, not the 'whole package'. Slowly this level of knowledge deteriorated, until people could no longer remember all the ways of doing, all the aspects of the creative trades. In the end, apprenticeships became very physical and demeaning processes. Apprentices were degraded and masters no longer knew how to be true mentors. It is now impossible to uncover the real stories, the original meanings for our arts and crafts. However, we can invent new meanings with our art - indeed we must. We can create new mythologies that include modern technologies. We need to re-discover how to be true mentors, how to pass on a skill in a way that encourages mutual aid rather than just creating clones from an original. A significant part of this task is the aweness that we are in a sense 're-inventing the wheel'. The damage to our knowledge and understanding of the deeper meaning of the arts has been done through hundreds of generations, through thousands of years.

To expect one generation to turn that all around is asking a great deal. However we need to strive towards this goal even though we know we will fail. In a sense by striving we have not failed. To strive is to be human. To want to help others is human, to use your skills and abilities to do so, is also very human. Artists need to strive to improve society, and maybe if we can do some of this work, the next generation will take it even further. Be the revolution that makes the revolution possible.

Chapter Four
The revolution that never happened...or did it?

Remarkably, through the industrial revolution, though a series of wars, famines, and destructive behaviour patterns, human beings have kept their creative traditions and practices alive. Despite the present relatively short term supremacy of science and logic - creativity, art and craft continues to flourish. We could have quite easily lost that function, and yet it is strong within each one of us still, and I believe it is on the increase - *'feel the force young Luke, it grows!'* **(sorry George Lucas)**

To create a theory about community arts and creative collaboration it is important to know the recent history of the arts as well. The present day community arts 'movement', if such a thing can be said to exist, has it's roots in the civil rights and feminist movements of the 1960's; the barricades in Paris; the development of pop music; and the growing awareness of the potential of community action. Creative activity was a part of those demonstrations and movements, it was often at the heart of civil disobedience- represented by the performing clowns, the musicians, the slogans on the walls, the peripheral but essential signs of the imminent revolution that never quite happened. Creativity wasn't the main cause, but it was always associated with the events, and as such was seen as an element of social change. Community art couldn't remain just an add-on to social action, it had to grow up, take on it's own form and character. In this way community art became a means to an end, and has continued to transform itself.

It is a feature of the new millennium that there are many jobs in the arts which we take for granted but which no one had heard of before the 1960's. These jobs were created from a youth culture and by young people who have now become middle aged, pensioners even, creating career paths that didn't exist beforehand. A good example is the job of DJ. The radio innovators of the 1960's became the dinosaurs of the 1990's, who had to be hacked away to allow in the next generation. In a way community artists are similar. We have created a career path which didn't exist beforehand, but its sustainability will be determined by whether we can pass this on as a going concern to the next generation.

I want to explain a little of what exactly we are passing on, also a little about what we aren't. I believe there is a cultural stereotype associated with an artist which is still prevalent, it can be summed up as follows: -

An individual artist creating art on his/her own, exhibiting it in a gallery/museum, being understood only by an intellectual minority. Basically, the artist, their work, their whole ethos, being narrow and secular. This applies throughout all arts disciplines - visual arts, crafts, dance, drama, music, video, photography, etc.

I believe that over the last thirty years a completely different type of artist has emerged, and their traits are as follows: -

Artists working collaboratively, in groups, making beautiful and understandable work. Working with community groups, enabling individuals and groups to express themselves,making memorials to their past and exploring their futures. This is occurring in all art forms and across the whole of Europe.

As I said earlier community arts has now become a multi-million pound industry with a very clear career path, structures, forms and organisations. Yet, the popular stereotype of 'the artist' remains the individualistic one. So, what to do?

All over the world right now artists are collaborating across art forms, using dance, drama, song, movement, visual arts, crafts, video, photography. Their work is different and vital. The main difference being it is undertaken in collaboration with people. These participants can be young children, youths, adults, adults with their children, or any variation on these. In addition these arts practitioners are working across many barriers, people with learning difficulties, visually impared, social disadvantage, 'those at risk', unemployed, etc. Community arts work can take on any issue - from the improvement of the environment, to health and history. Projects have a tendency to meander, add bits, and take on a life of their own. Community arts work is never just a simple task leading to a simple product, but that is why it is so much fun. This has meant it has been, and remains, difficult to identify a community arts project. Many people have been involved in arts projects that they have claimed as community art, but which weren't! The following are examples from the visual arts to illustrate arts activities which are not community arts, but they apply across all art forms.

** An individual artist doing their own work getting shows in Galleries.*

This is not community art.

** Art in Public- 'dog turds on the piazza' artists being commissioned to create work in public places.*

Unfortunately, some of these art works have been sited in very densely populated areas, away from the outsides of corporate areas. They have sometimes caused offence and created many problems for genuine community artists.

**There are now any number of artists-in-residence- resident in schools, youth clubs, community centres, prisons, hospitals, a fantastic diversity of situations and institutions.*

A lot of these are brilliant community artists working on a wide range of fantastic projects, however some are just continuing their own work, but allowing ‘mere mortals’ to watch them do it.

**There are now many specialist community artists groups and organisations.*
I know these are doing the work

There is also a large amount of applied creativity coming from community arts groups, community development projects, voluntary groups, and any number of other sources. The Easterhouse project in Glasgow created a great arts project which was very contentious in the 1980’s. Many said it was great community art, others claimed it wasn’t art at all. Judge for yourselves. The estate contains over 50,000 people no launderette, few shops, but the busiest Bookmaker in Europe. Some residents decided to re-create a Butlin’s holiday camp on the estate for a week, to get away from their circumstances, have a good time, and generally let their hair down. So they had tons of sand brought in, made palm trees, decorated the main square, dressed up as Red Coats and had a fantastic time. They raised enough money from the project to pay for the creation of a launderette on the estate. Was this great art with a purpose, the application of creativity and imagination to better people’s lives, or was it just pandering to the lowest common denominator?

For me, this was a great example of creativity and it’s application within a community setting. When we restrict ourselves to just making an art work with a group of children, we are doing them and ourselves a disservice, we can do so much more. I have for many years ‘just’ made art with people, but despite that I have created many incidental and accidental community transformations.

Chapter Five
High art is an intimidating force

Over the past hundreds of years in Western Europe art has been seen as something additional, as a frivolous add-on. This denies it's actual importance and place in our society as I have explained over the past chapters. Instead, it has tended to become the preserve of the rich and the powerful. They have historically used art to show how superior they are, to celebrate their achievements, and most importantly to show how extravagant they can be. This started in the Egyptian,Greek and Roman and traditions. It carried on into the patronage of the Middle Ages, and to the present day patronage of art and artists by those that can afford them. Opera is a wonderful art, but it is viewed mostly by the rich, those that can afford it, and those that think they understand it.

Hand in hand with this patronage is a process of intellectualisation. As the arts and crafts have withdrawn themselves from the streets into the drawing rooms and the chateaux, they have accrued kudos and status. The justifications which the rich used for their patronage were the building blocks for the present disciplines of art history and art theory. The rich had to explain why they supported certain artists and not others, so they gave meanings and significance to the works created, some of which were superfluous, and not even intended by the artists.

The last 300 years or so has increased this intellectualization of the arts. The present day galleries and museums have done little to unravel the mystifications which have been created - in a sense they hang on to them with delight. This applies in all disciplines, from music, through the arts and crafts, into writing, film and every creative field.

"The characteristic element of contemporary art from a sociological point of view is the fact that contemporary art divides the public into two groups of people: those who understand it, and those that don't." Ortega y Gasset

This process has not helped the public image of art or artists. They are dismissed or ignored by the majority of people, and as they strive to be taken seriously the cultural disdain for their work continues. Artists need to break out of this cycle.

There is a high art argument about the 'watering down' of art when it is made accessible, but I can not agree with it. By making your art accessible you are not having to compromise your imagination or creativity. Accessible art is accessible through it's situation; how it is shown; through it's attitude to it's audience; not condescending. Accessible art does not have to be simple. Great art will, and always does, move people, it communicates with them. Whoever they are, whatever their language, wherever they come from, great art will win through. Poor art, illl conceived and poorly presented art, will always struggle, will always be misunderstood and ignored. We need more imaginative, creative and accessible art being made. Accessible doesn't equate with poor quality or being reduced in quality.

To criticize the current arts world for its excesses and its badly managed publicity is easy. The criticism by the popular press of Carl André and his bricks, or Damien Hirst and his sheep is well known. However, such vacuous and simplistic attacks do not address the hole at the very core of the high art system. This hole is the way in which art has been given a 'higher' significance, it's intellectual value. Creativity needs to be inclusive and expansive. Creativity is an internal force which everyone has, can understand, and can access. This is the plug which fills the gap at the centre of the art world.

"Building myths about the artists-as-creative genius serves only to remove art from the community, to keep it in silent rooms where visitors come and wonder if they understand."*vi

Fashions in the arts change over time. Some artists are 'in' and then they go 'out' only to be 'discovered' many years later. This is not to say that only art history follows this cycle. One can easily observe the same process in science. All sciences, be they physics, mathematics, whatever, are evolving processes. They flex, and change and the aspects which come into view depend on the awareness of the interpreter. As Stephen Hawking relates in his book *"A Brief History of Time"* science is trying to reveal the whole shape of a human being, but only has a big toe to work from. I believe art historians are similarly trying to justify their theories through the examination of a 'big toe'. This misses out on the fabulous pleasure of the whole human body – they are preoccupied with intellectual interpretation of inanimate paintings, rather than 'doing' art. Creativity and art are free spirits. They can not be defined easily or given an easily agreed title. When we are really in touch with our creativity we just 'do it' whatever it is, and it is only in retrospect that we can justify it or theorise about it.

In my own work I am seeking to express and impart my own passion, something which I feel has been left out of the modern high art experience. I find most exhibitions very soulless, distanced, very intellectualized. Indeed they can afford to be this way, because a very small percentage of our population ever enter a gallery door. If it were high quality and accessible, this would change. The art I and many other make doesn't rely on the patronage of a museum, so we can have it out on the streets, where everyone can see it. The creativity I want to promote should be at the heart of a culture an integral part of everyday experience, and as such needs to be powerful and effective. Community art has started to do just that, it has now made some really effective, accessible monuments to community change, and the power of local people throughout Britain. It makes people smile every day as they pass by. Let alone the influence on the individual who took part in the collaborative making of such art. Creativity of this kind changes people's lives, influences their decisions in later life, and makes people feel in touch with the wider world. I know that this art has touched some people in a very profound way, and has effected them in a truly self-revelatory manner. This is a wonderful process, and it needs to be shared and expanded. Mostly it can only ever be experienced first hand- *"You had to be there"*. Often words do not do the experience justice and can not describe its intensity or depth.

One of the main aims of just about every artistic movement, every manifesto from artists, is to be seen as a force for change. All artists want to be taken seriously and be seen as being of significance. From the Impressionists through to the Britpop artists there is a self-conscious belief that their particular art is important and deserves serious consideration. Almost all new artists' manifestos over the past two hundred years have been met with ridicule and scorn by the 'public', by the media and by the vast majority of society. Community art offers an alternative to this way of viewing the arts; it is powerful and transformative for individuals; it does bring about social change. This is art as a means of self-improvement and inspiration, art which is ahead of its time rather than trying to be noticed by being wacky.

Of course I would say that wouldn't I? But I'm not alone in having this view, and it has been around for a very long time. What follows is a statement from 1978, and shows a good grasp of the main issues and needs for art at that time, which still apply today.

1 we are increasingly dissatisfied with the failure of so much contemporary art to communicate with anyone outside a small circle of initiates.
2 we believe too many artists are content with the public's view that modern art only fulfills a minor function within society.
3 we refuse to accept that art today must inevitably be regarded as a marginal, mercantile and misunderstood activity alienated from most members of its potential audience.
4 we are convinced that art must be transformed into a progressive force for change in the future.
5 we consider that the artist ought to engage with as many as possible of the working people who think art has nothing to do with them.
6 we insist that art should have everything to do with them, because it cannot sustain itself without a central involvement with the life we all live now.
7 we want artists to help create an egalitarian society by developing new ways of reaching towards the many rather than the few.
8 we maintain that artists should become responsive to the broad-based contexts in which they must operate, because most people rightly recoil from attempts to impose on them an art they do not want.
9 we would like society to regard artists as having an active part to play in dealing with the human, social and political issues, which affect everyone's existence.
10 we declare that art needs people as much as people need art: the two should be inextricably linked with each other, and never divorced so damagingly again. *vii

Amazingly,high art *needs* to be peripheral to mainstream culture. By not being taken seriously in the mainstream they can remain inert, and in the control of the few. At present, the system is safe because no one cares enough to question it. Art historians can perpetuate their myths safe in the knowledge that they will be unquestioned.

These myths take various forms: -

**Artists are geniuses, not like us*

**There is no job called "Artist"*

**There is no career path, there is no expectation of employment*

**There is a link between poverty and creativity*

**You must be able to intellectualize your work, you must explain it through it's connectedness to art history*

For me, artists need to be seen to be just like you and me, we need to be part of the mainstream, and not thought of as 'geniuses' or intellectuals.

There is definately a job called 'artist', there are also many other jobs, called 'community artist', 'art therapist', 'artist in the community', 'arts administrator', they all have value and are now recognised.

There is now a very well worn track from study into full time employment, I have made it, and so have many hundreds of others.

There is a myth about 'being an artist' which asserts that you should be poor, and how this enables you to create great art. Why should all creative people have to suffer in a materialistic culture? Indeed there is good evidence that being able to sustain yourself in terms of food, clothing and other essentials can greatly improve your creativity. You are able to focus your mind and concentrate on being creative, free from fear and worries.

Community artists don't need to explain their work in terms of dead artists.

When art is truly collaborative, when art is made as a whole, it transcends the mundane and becomes more than the sum of its parts. These are the fundamental differences between 'high art' and 'community art'. Good art/creativity does not have to relate to art history, famous artists. It can just 'be'. Indeed great art is created in the moment and does not have to be given meaning. Good art does not have to be explained in an intellectual way. As Frank Stella said...

"What you see is what you see."

Chapter Six
Where is my community?

"The rapidity with which the human mind changes and with which the human, through his technology, makes his own world into something completely different from what, just a short while ago, it was, is so great that, for all practical purposes, the pace of evolutionary development, when compared to it, is standing still." *viii

Community no longer exists in the form in which it did fifty years ago, or even twenty years ago. However the 'golden age' of our memories is also an illusion. There was no time when child abuse didn't exist or the rich did not exploit the poor, certainly not in the last two thousand years. These have been constants, but change has always been implicit within communities. Every community has changed radically. This change has been national, international and global. Every community is now unrecognizable from how it was in 1950, little has been left intact. The effects of globalization, and the creation of a New World Order has swept us all up in a recent process of rapid change. But this process has been on-going for thousands of years. Our cities and towns have been radically transformed in the past twenty years. It's taken a bit longer to affect the smaller rural communities of Britain, but we are now all in advanced stages of change that will be irreversible.

We can all either mourn its passing and get on with trying to create something new; or we can cling to an idealized view of the past (whatever it was), and bemoan any changes which we experience as affecting our lives. In urban settings changes have really come about with the raising of boundaries between houses. Terraced houses afforded very little privacy - thin walls, outdoor toilets, children playing in the streets, meant that people knew what you were doing. We have chosen to move away from that into detached housing with large walls, fences and defenses which are supposed to deter burglars, but which deter much more. In rural settings the biggest change has been the influx of outsider (in my community in West Wales it has been the English). In all places there are identifiable 'insiders' and 'outsiders'. The openness and inclusivity of the 'insiders' will either deter or encourage participation by the 'outsiders'. The 'insiders' need to be secure in the knowledge that by including others they will enhance the experience of all. This is always a risk, but in present times where change is an integral part of all our lives, we have really no alternatives. Change within our communities will always bring disturbance; it is only how we view these changes which determines whether we experience them as 'good' or 'bad'.

Over the past years there have been many attempts to bring about change 'from above' by architects, town planners and local authorities. Mostly these have been disasters, because the instigators of change have not taken into consideration the needs of people who live in the area which is to be changed. This process can be seen in attempts to change the face of estates in London, Glasgow, or other large cities. Time and again they are identified as being concentrations of crime, drugs and other social evils, and time and again they have been targeted for change by architects, planners and the like. I am not criticizing such professionals for attempting to improve the lot of people living in conditions of deprivation, but if the so-called 'experts' attempt this change without true inclusion of the local people it will be doomed to failure.

We need to learn the lesson that a 'sense of place' or 'community pride' can not be imposed. Community consultation needs to be taken seriously. Too often it has been a token exercise, too often the local people have actually had the knowledge and means to change their lives for the better, but they have been ignored and marginalised. Good community consultation desperately needs creativity, because questionnaires will very infrequently be answered fully. The people who live on disadvantaged housing estates are the ones who know what is wrong with the environment. They have an intimate knowledge of the failings of their environment and their needs, so we need to include them. But do they know how to bring about change, or what is achievable? This is where a community consultation process which includes specialist expertise – planners, architects, artists, social workers, the full gambit – can ensure that local people can make imaginative leaps in their plans and expectations. Specialist experts in this area of work need to be passing on their knowledge, not retaining it for themselves. Often an architect will not allow local people to use their creativity and imagination, often planners won't contemplate informing local people about what is possible. Consultation must be long term and not a temporary inconvenience for the 'important' people.

Unfortunately, there have been some terrible examples of arts projects, which have used consultation with the community as a 'token' means of gaining support for public sculptures or other art works. This process mainly happens through Arts Agencies who allow small groups of individuals to sit and look at various artists' work and 'judge' which would be the best one for a site. Often this takes the form of an exhibition of design proposals in a public place, which 'the public' can vote on. This approach just perpetuates the 'dog turd on the piazza' syndrome of artists making abstract sculptures which bear no relationship to the place, the people or the history of the community. Too often such work is called 'community art'. It is not, it is just the outcome of a process of manipulation and condescension.

Poor art practice is never excusable, but community art has often found itself involved in very questionable projects. Not always through willful manipulation, but more often through the political games of local authorities and stakeholder corporations. This approach manifested itself in the process of artists being employed to paint murals on buildings that were eyesores or temporary projects in order to placate tenants. A phrase emerged in the 1970's, which described this type of work as *"Community artists papering over the cracks in society"*. I know that on occasions I have been used this way, just about all of the artists I know have been subjected to this kind of pressure. They wanted to be employed, the local authorities had funding - it is hard to resist and certainly such situations are never black and white. There will always be those authorities who manipulate the arts for their own ends. But at all times we can try to involve local people in as much as possible, attempting to ensure that the community is participating as fully in the process and product.

This can lead us to look at what we describe as a 'community'. How small is a community. What is 'local'? A community can be one of interests, of geography, of just about everything and anything. As someone who works with communities, I do not restrict myself to just geographical groupings, because in that way I miss out on a lot of interesting opportunities. This approach really sums up the new 'creative community' – where community art is not just restricted to 'areas of high social need', not just 'papering over the cracks'. In the beginning community artists wanted to only work in working class communties. If we free ourselves from the delusion that they still exist, our work can become a more mature and inclusive process. Our understanding of the word 'community' needs now to be much more complex. Community has changed and we must adapt our work to suit the new circumstances. I like the following as a simple definition of community:

** Community is inclusive. Individual differences are celebrated. Soft individualism, rather than rugged, can flourish.*

** Community is realistic and multi-dimensional. Each member is free to experience his or her own facet of reality.*

** Community facilitates healing once its members stop trying to heal or fix one another.*

** Community is reflective, contemplative and introspective.*

** A community's members can fight gracefully.*

** A community is a group of all leaders who share equal responsibility for and commitment to maintaining its spirit.*

** A community is a highly effective work group.*

** A community is the ideal consensual decision making body.*

** In a community a wide range of gifts and talents is celebrated.*

The Foundation for Community Encouragement, Inc.

Surely, this points to the way forward. I worked with a group of ex-miners in South Wales, one of whom was in his eighties - a fantastic storyteller and a natural stand-up comedian - one of his little tales was as follows.

"I remember sitting on the curb of the street with a stick, poking it into the gutter. We used to do that as kids, poke sticks all over the place, but mostly down gutters! Anyway, I'm sitting there, poking my stick, when all of a sudden this huge shadow looms over me. There's a huge man looking down at me, he looks me in the face and he says 'I don't know you, but I know your Da, and your Da's Da'."

This was his community, there was recognition of family, place and belonging all tied up in that one statement. It must have been wonderful to have belonged, and to have felt so included. It was lovely, but there were also disadvantages in living in such a community - exploitation of children, high child mortality rates, exploitation of workers, danger and disease. Was it such a good place? It's all about change and about perspectives.

Chapter Seven

Impossible aspirations

I have explored the depth and the diversity of how the arts have been used and viewed in the past. Now I want to address some of the issues which are arising in the present. Reflecting the cultural situation in Britain and Europe, and how that influences the work of community artists. As stated, the arts have traditionally been funded through elitist patronage. This has led to a mind orientated culture and society. It comes from the increased significance Western culture has given to science, maths and the other 'new' subjects. There is seen to be no room for creativity in a world ruled by science. A culture which is dominated by 'facts' tends to see creativity and the arts as 'fictions'.

We need to reassert the true nature of creativity – to bring to the fore the impact and social change which can occur when creativity is aligned with social collaboration. The past thirty or so years have seen a re-discovery of some of these truths, and this is encouraging. Thirty years ago there was no funding available for community art. Now its importance and significance is recognised in the millions of pounds available through Lottery funding in Britain, which is specifically targeting participatory arts activities. Unfortunately, as with all arts funding, such support comes with strings attached, and the recent years have seen additional strings and conditions. If these conditions had been added by experienced practitioners, I wouldn't be so worried, but they seem to have been attached by accountants and administrators who tend to stifle or put a different emphasis on artistic practice. This has created a numbers-orientated approach to describing and measuring community arts - creativity by numbers. The need for practitioners to include as many participants as possible in their activities in order to show 'value for money' to funders can be very divisive. Many young community artists are involved in number crunching projects from the start, and it takes them many years to unravel the imposed administrative restraints, to see the pure essence of what it is they are doing. When they do achieve this unravelling, community artists recognise the core principle of creative collaboration to be a belief in the innate ability of all human beings to be creative and collaborative. This is a very political and socially charged contention. It leads to people changing their lives, sometimes breaking down and crying, sometimes laughing, but generally sorting themselves out. Indeed such a belief needs to be held in order for community arts work to be effective, and when we hold such a belief we actually are striving towards something which is impossible.

I believe the natural state of someone who is being both creative and collaborative is to aspire to change society. Those that do this are seen as visionaries, as dreamers in today's scientific culture. But, by dreaming and visioning they are actually creating the future, they are making these wishes come about. I know this to be true because I had dreams and visions of being able to work full time as a community artist over twenty years ago, and this is what happened. At that time if I had described the funding, the diversity of projects, and the range of support structures for such work that currently exists, I would have been laughed at and derided as a fantasist. This is a hugely important part of creative collaboration. When we spark our own creativity and the creativity of others, we communicate, we gather strength, we mutually assist, and then the world around us changes. We influence the world by being infused with possibilities, and when we rest and try to keep hold of what we have achieved we allow inertia to set in. Creative collaboration is about potential for the future, and as such we will always be seen as impossible dreamers. But we would rather be that than perpetuators of the establishment view.

In a sense, creative collaboration and community art was dreamed up by humanity as a whole. As such it is perpetually changing and diversifying. Just to prove it, I found a copy of an article written in 1985 by ***Judith Steyn and Brian Sedgemore***. It made me sit up and take notice. Here is a brief extract: -

"The concept of community art is a dead one. In its time community art was a useful expression of activism, it was often politically speculative, and challenged the notion of the passive consumer. Now not only has activism given way to professionalism, but the state has appropriated the very art that was meant to 'storm citadels.'

Rather than trying to resurrect it, we should redefine work, and accept art as part of the process of material production – whilst rejecting the notion of art as a commodity. Instead of giving artists charity, or grants at national or local level, we should move to a system of commissioning works for the community."

This may come as a surprise to people that Community Art had already died in 1985. It makes me wonder what I have been doing ever since! In a sense the article is correct. That particular style of community art is dead. The politically active; the revolutionary stance; the *do it for love not money* attitude has become professionalised, and that is not a bad thing. I think we actually achieved a great deal of the vision for the future that was contained in the article, in a sense the revolution happened even though no-one noticed!

However, there is a truth here that relates to our relationship to community art. For many of us when we first start working in community art, it is like being in love - it is intense, vibrant, and a great deal of energy is expended. As community art has matured and grown up, so individuals who are involved have realised that it is a long-term relationship.

The urgency and frenzy of the early years give way to a more steady and respectful pace. Community art is always greater than the sum of its participants. Each new person gives an added impetus and vitality to community art and we need to accommodate both stages- those young impetuous lovers and the mature plodders. However just because I may be a mature plodder doesn't mean I can't have aspirations and visions!

What are the new visions, the new challenges?

Passing it on

We need to ensure that the next generation of practitioners claim ownership of community art. The only way we can make that happen is not be too prescriptive, but to allow the next generations of artists to move community art into new areas and into new ways of creating. As one of the 'old guard' I have to be wary of saying that my way is best. Maybe my way was the best way at that time, but there are other things happening now. Community art can not afford to stand still and admire itself, or it will run the risk of disappearing up it's own backside!

Defining our practice

'Community art' contains two of the most misunderstood words in the English language. Thus far there has never been an adequate definition of what community art is; of where participation starts and ends; of the role and practice of public consultation? There needs to be a clearer description of how good work can become great; and how to look beyond the immediate problems of fund raising and satisfying the requirements of the Arts Council. Community art has to bite the bullet and start making qualitative judgements of its value as well as quantitative ones. Concentrating on measuring the numbers of participants and the time it takes to allow them to 'participate' has forced us into assessing and judging work in a very limited way. With a more qualitative approach the process and product can be judged in terms of where the participants started and where they ended (i.e. what change was experienced by them) in the following areas:

* expectations
* self awareness
* group identity
* understanding of arts materials and techniques

These evaluation categories will then help to define the work, ensure that the value of community arts practice is recognised beyond sheer numbers of participants and time restrictions.

Defending our territory

Community art has developed a good reputation, and nowadays it is 'worthy'. Suddenly all art in public places is participatory, with the advent of Lottery Art For All, many artists are assuming community artists' clothing. By defining our practice we can clearly identify those who are doing the work and those who aren't. We can distinguish between those arts organisations which are true community motivators and stimulators, and those that have appointed a token 'education' officer.

Proper training

To be a community artist is to have a clear career path. Unlike fine art or these other confused arts degrees, a career in community art is well defined. Many artists now claim to be community artists, but in fact they aren't. They don't have very much idea of the theory or the practice of community arts. They need to be challenged in their assumptions, and need to really understand what community art is about. Unfortunately, there are very few community arts courses. There are lots that pretend to be and many that aspire to be. However there is a huge gap in the market. Community artists are not a product of a fine art or music degree; they actually can not be created through such study. Community artists may well have trained in fine art, but it is only when they combine this knowledge with at least two or three years in the real world that they become community artists. But, even then, they may never actually grasp what it is to be a community artist. I'm attempting to define the indefinable, so I'll stop!

Aspirations for the future

* *We need to promote community art. We need to trumpet our achievements. We need to make a big fuss. I know it is not in our nature, but there is a need to respond to the above mentioned stereotypes and misperceptions.*

* *Living as I do in West Wales I would like to encourage community artists to think in terms of rural as well as urban practice. I know there is a huge amount of work still to be done in urban communities, but community art also needs to address the very different and specialised problems which are represented in our rural communities.*

* *We need to look beyond these shores and develop a European perspective. We need to see what is happening out there, gain knowledge about it and pass it on. There is always a paradox in terms of community art, in that we should be focused on our own community, but at the same time be outward looking.*

* *We need to see that community art can lead to community development and action. All too often our work has been restricted by factors such as: our own*

lack of vision; the lack of vision of the funders; the lack of time and money; our lack of confidence and ability. We can afford to aspire to community change through creativity, because we now have the expertise and knowledge to be able to achieve it. If we combine this expertise with taking risks we might still be around in 20 years time.

* *We need to fund our work from a much wider range of sources. The present reliance on the Arts Council and Lottery is dangerous. The links between community art and community development are now so strong that we should be receiving funds from Social Services, the Health Authorities, Community Regeneration, etc.*

Community art is dead, long live community art, long may it diversify, long may it change and evolve.

Chapter Eight
The career path of the future

We need to be visionaries, and we need to challenge the establishment through dreaming. Whether any of the visions come true is another matter, but I believe we are well on the way towards realising many. **"Use or Ornament? The Social Impact of participation in the Arts"** by Francois Matarasso has been very helpful in terms of quantifying and listing the value of community arts work. This has helped to increase the understanding of such work, but it is still not completely clear just how powerful community art is. The use of the word 'participation' has become endemic amongst arts adminstrators, and unfortunately it covers a multitude of sins. Short term projects which are just about allowing children a brief glimpse of art or an artist is participation of a kind. Whilst people are able to participate they can be kept in the place of the student rather than teacher. I believe really liberating and good community art, enables those participating to not only gain in confidence but to liberate themselves from their own limitations. It enables those participating to fully appreciate who they are, and how strong they can be. This is a learning process not just for them, but for the artist who is facilitating such a project.

Unfortunately, most people's expectations of creativity are pretty limited. Even those trained and grounded in the arts actually undervalue the effects of their work and are unaware of the potential that they carry. Most communities have a limited view of creativity, and will tend to be attracted to what they can see, what they know and what has been done before. There is a lack of innovation in terms of community development when it comes to arts activities, mainly I believe because we have all just scratched the surface of what is possible. It will probably be another twenty years (at least) before creativity is understood for what it actually is, and what it can achieve. This will only come about if community artists continue to stretch and expand their practice, if we continue to be innovative and don't sit on our laurels. By their very nature, good community artists will ensure that this happens, because when we truly work in a creative and collaborative process it is permanently in a state of change. I am filled with hope for the future, because organizations and individuals all around Britain and Europe are now facing the kinds of challenges we all dreamed about 20 years ago. We are working on large scale long term projects which are the kind of work we would have given our right arm for ten years ago, but the world and probably the artists weren't ready for them then. Now community artists are prepared and capable, and I am confident that they can create highly innovative and creative work.

There is now a clearly defined career path for community artists from adventure playgrounds to residencies, and I'd suggest that it typically follows these steps:

1 Working with many participants for little money and few materials - Adventure Playgrounds, Summer Playschemes, Adult Education, Adult Training, etc. Short term, lots of stress, children mostly, basic skills.

2 Working with fewer participants and with more money - Day Care Centres, Life-long Learning, Short term School Projects, Residents Groups, etc. Smaller groups, more intensity, learning, more passing on of skills, better pay, better materials.

3 Working for longer periods of time - Schools residencies, Hospitals, Tenants Groups, OAP Centres, etc. Having time, money, space and the ability to communicate more complex skills.

4 Working Full Time - community arts organizations, Integrated Hospital residencies, Community Development, etc. Starting to understand the long-term implications, using a variety of skills and materials, a wide range of participants. Having your Tax and NI paid.

These four stages of a career in community arts are linked in terms of who you work with, how long you work with them and how much you are paid. On the ideal career path, the numbers worked with reduce as the length of time and amount paid increases. So, how do we make sure that people understand and see that community arts is a relevant and useful thing to do?

As a species we need to understand what it is to be collaborative. The exact nature of collaboration is in the sharing of responsibility, and our openness to criticism and change. In the beginning of community arts, during the 1960's, there was a kind of blind belief in the power of the co-operative with everything shared and everything equal. Usually it did not work. It is now recognised that there needs to be structure, a framework and responsibilities. However, to be authoritarian and dictatorial is going to the other extreme. There is a middle way in which a process is controlled and led, whilst allowing change to happen, encouraging people to grow at their own pace, and to develop their strengths. This middle way needs to be propagated and given more credence. Unfortunately Western Europe is not a 'hot bed' of such activity. We have founded our culture on a pyramidal power structure. Art can be one of the driving forces to find alternatives. We could use creativity to generate systems of business which are democratic and engender change. Business for community benefit which share their profits to other new innovations rather than keeping it all. That's a worthy aim for the next twenty years or so, along with so many others!

Creativity is there to create new ways of being. Through using our imaginations we will create new ways of interacting, and one of the main features of these has to be the integration of collaboration. Most arts have been an individualistic practice for the last two hundred years. Through separating and isolating the individual artists it has actually weakened those individuals. There is a real lesson which has to be learnt. When we collaborate, it makes individuals stronger, not weaker. Paradoxically when we act in accord with others we find our identity, our individuality. When we work in a team we actually find out who we are, more than by being isolated or working on our own. Once we have come to terms with this truth, we can then implement the following steps.

* *We need to encourage artist led initiatives and get away from administrator led organizations by encouraging self-help amongst artists, craftspeople, dancers, etc.*

* *We need to have community-based initiatives, which promote local activities, not just the arts in isolation, but linking art into housing, community development, farming, power generation, and lots of other things.*

* *We need to have creative people mutually supporting each other, not just looking after their own interests but spreading information, sharing details and encouraging each other.*

* *Let's push the boundaries of creativity, into business, into sports, into all aspects of our lives.*

* *We all need to understand the difference between high art and community art. The theoretical and practical*

differences need to be spelled out, discussed and then understood - not only by practitioners, but also by arts funders, local authorities, and everyone involved.

* *We need to encourage the Arts Council to address the historical anomalies within it's revenue funding of clients. Most large scale institutions are loss making white elephants, and there are many young thrusting organisations which need the support of the Arts Council, but can't receive it. The Arts Council needs to set up a risk fund, possibly funded by a half a percentage cut in their major revenue clients. This would create a huge new pool of funding. The new clients would be given three years risk money, told to go out, and see if it works. They would also need to 'mentored' by either an experienced individual in their field or an organisation. If at the end of the three years they were doing well they could then become a revenue client.*

* *Most community arts organisations are such young guns, they are dynamic, break-even organisations with a great future. They need to continue to show the older, more established organisations how to be financially reliable.*

* *Community art needs to stop being reliant on the Lottery for so much of its funding. It needs to find a broader range of supporters for such activities, and win their confidence and financial support. We need to win the support of Social Services, the Health Service, all the other agencies that are actually interested in community art and development, but don't fund the activities one hundred percent.*

* *Doctors prescribing arts courses rather than pills; disruptive children being sent on drama and dance projects; they're already nearly here and they need to be encouraged.*

There's a lot of work to do before this comes about, but there are already small examples of this presently being practiced. Hospitals are now recognizing the therapeutic value of art, the healing process can be speeded up by providing a warm and welcoming environment. Offenders can be encouraged to find jobs by having the chance to express themselves, and by finding their internal motivation. It all boils down to whether we want to continue looking for short-term solutions, or if we can use our imaginations to see the bigger picture.

A new phrase has arisen with the new millennium - *"Creative Industries"*, I know it is easy to be cynical about New Labour and their sound-bites, but I guess we have to accept that this is the way forward. If artists and creative people all believe that they are part of an industry, then we might actually start working collaboratively. I know that where I live the number of jobs in what can be loosely termed the '*Cultural Creative Industry*' far outnumber any other industry. Where agriculture was once the main income generator, culture and tourism have taken over. If we can attract tourists ,and encourage local people to participate in, good quality creative products and companies. Those with an understanding and sympathy for local history and place, then we will be getting somewhere. If the creative industries could become a powerful lobbyist for their own interests and for the promotion of good quality arts and crafts, then local Authorities, Government Departments and the E.U. will start to sit up and listen. Eventually, fund creativity schemes in all their diversity. Indeed the projections are that the creative industries are to continue to develop over the next twenty years, and may well become the most economically significant in Britain.

So, there is a great opportunity for all creative people. We will only reap the benefits of this when creative people start behaving with respect and responsibility towards themselves and the future of their work. Let's stop seeing divisions and differences. Let's work towards the long-term future, which has to have a healthy collaborative creative core in order for it to survive.

Lets remember art is more powerful than money, it lasts longer, and can change people's lives. Human beings have been creative and collaborative since the beginning of time. Money, celebrity and fame are just short-term goals. The whole of our present Western culture is based on a misunderstanding and a slant towards individualism. Capitalism and the ideals of materialism will inevitably crumble. It is up to all of us to make sure that the culture which replaces this one is better, more sustainable, more beautiful, and more precious. Everyone needs to be creative and collaborate right now for the sake of tomorrow.

Chapter Nine
Creativity and health

It is now widely acknowledged that there is a direct correlation between sport and health. If you are active in a sport or physical activity it can increase your health, improve your physical condition, and this is something we see as being beneficial. Indeed, it can lengthen your life and make you more beautiful! With this in mind there has been a proliferation of Sports and Leisure Centres throughout Britain; the television and media promotes a wide range of support systems; businesses and promotional centres have burgeoned; it has become a major industry. In addition, we have created another huge industry which is developing our awareness of food, our diet, and the way this affects our well being, our confidence and our self image.

Whilst not wanting to detract from it all, there is also a down side. Individuals can do themselves great damage through focusing on such issues, some have become obsessive, in isolation this can cause problems. My interest is to develop creativity as an ally to the sport and health industries, to increase the focus on creativity, and to ensure that people are made aware of the potential benefits of allying sport, healthy eating and creativity.

We all know there are strong links between the stimulation of creativity and well being, in terms of individual awareness, health, compassion and understanding. If we ally this with physical activities and healthy eating, we are on the way to becoming a proper human being. Too often individuals have focused on one aspect of this more holistic approach. Many people try to diet, try to loose weight through various forms of eating - only protein - whatever. However, if they are unhappy with their lives, if they lead sedentiary lives infront of the television, they are bound to fail. In our present culture we are seeking happiness without realising that there are a diversity of ways of attaining it. We are programmed to think if we do one thing - go on a diet, do aerobics, yoga, whatever - it will radically change our lives. We need to comprehend that there is more to life than a quick fix. What I am suggesting is individuals need to undertake a far wider range of activities which could include creativity, good and sensible food, physical exercise. Such a combined programme would lead to emotional and mental stimulation which can develop a good relationship to your body, mind and soul. This could develop into programmes for individuals, schools, businesses and corporations, and create wider community benefits.

Individuals

If an individual is involved in such a mixed programme on a regular basis, it can lead to any of the following:-

** Increased confidence and self awareness*

** Increased energy, increased enthusiasm, increased vigour*

** Personal empowerment and development*

** A sense of identity and place in society*

** A move away from being bored and cynical towards becoming enthusiastic and participatory*

** You will live longer!*

** You will use your brain*

A creative person is being stimulated in a positive manner which will increase their resistance to illness, this has a long term benefit in terms of developing well being in our society. Especially, when creativity is linked to physical activities and other stimulations, creativity can be a very important part of an overall plan. This kind of programme will lead to happier individuals, who will feel fulfilled and content. It reduces the amount of time they'll spend in front of the television, or feeling sorry for themselves. The knock on effects of such a programme would drastically reduce the drain on the National Health Service; reduce the consumption of anti-depressants; reduce violence; and promote tolerance in the society as a whole.

Schools

What if we were to teach our children how to be happy? How to enjoy life, to be creative, physically active, and eat good healthy food. Children would learn a lot faster, be able to work collaboratively, and would spend more time being of use to others. How would that affect our society? If we were to make such goals the aim of the educational system, particularly the early years, it would radically change the way in which people behaved in the future. Instead of schools being production lines, places to incarcerate miscreants, they would be the greenhouses for the future, the way schools were intended to be.

Business and corporations

If combined workshops were run for businesses and corporations, where the benefits of combining creativity with good diet and physical exercise were promoted. These could take the form of participatory workshops for weekends or weeks; mentoring and year long programmes; visits from inspirational talkers and organisations.

** This will create ownership, a sense of pride, and a historical context for the company*
** The workers will become more productive*
** They will bond and collaborate well*
** They will enjoy going to work*
** They will put more into work, they will come up with creative and productive ideas*
** If managment are able to not feel threatended by such ideas, then the whole company can advance and develop organically*

I know this all sounds like pie in the sky. It is. But, I really don't see any other viable alternatives being promoted at present. Indeed, I don't think these are radical or progressive enough, I would advise even more. The culture in which we live is stagnating, we are desperately unhappy, unhealthy, sick, and growing fatter by the day. What are the radical schemes being offered to change this?

The National Health Service creaks and groans, it is over run, so, they build more hospitals. That is not the solution. Why are the people so sick in the first place, they don't exercise enough, they eat the wrong food, they are unhappy. Why do they do all those things when they know they are wrong? Because we are offering them a very limited world view, because they are in unhappy jobs.

The roads system is now starting to get gridlocked. The solution offered is to build bigger and more motorways. That is not the solution. Why do people feel they have to drive their own cars all the time, why do people identify themselves with their car? What are the effects of the intense advertising and promotional industry, allied to the motor industry? Why don't people want to use public transport? How can we change perceptions.

Individually and collectively we are powerful, we can offer alternatives, we can develop radical solutions. Individually and collectively we can create the next ways of being, indeed, it is down to us, successive governments have only ever offered short term solutions. The next years will be critical in terms of how the planet evolves, how human beings are seen in the distant future. We are either a virus which is infecting the planet at present and is about to self destruct and destroy itself. Or, we will be remembered as being able to adapt, change and evolve, despite almost bringing about the collapse of the whole planet. I know where I want to go!

Practical Creative Collaboration

Chapter Ten
Work on yourself

Every human being has an imagination, and they use it every moment of the day, as well as during their sleep. The imagination leads us to visions, ideas, and the potential for change. If we apply creativity- we manifest our inspirations- they actually happen. When we use our creativity with others in a collaborative manner, we can overcome social problems, create massive monuments, indeed civilisation is a testimony to creative collaboration. This is the foundation from which the creative collaboration theory stems. Without an understanding of this, art will always be individualistic and coming from the ego. Unfortunately, the connection between intellect and creativity, which has come from the art historical theories, restricts artists and encourages them to work on their own, as an intellectual. This myth is not true, you do not need to work on your own, you can work with others, as I said, everyone is creative.

We all act as channels for our own creativity. Often the inspiration for great art comes from the unknown. Indeed most people who have made an impact on the world have created their theories and their artifacts from outside the norm. That is why they are remarkable. Artists of all kinds have this ability, to step outside the expected, and to create things that are awe inspiring. When asked where their inspiration came from, many will reply *"I don't know, it was just a dream, a thought"*. This is a very important point. In order to be creative we need to clear our minds of the clutter and every day matters to allow the inspiration to come through. If we are dealing with the mundane details, combined with worries and fears, we are not being a channel for the inspiring, we are just playing at it. As individuals we need to become a good 'channel', and this takes preparation. The preparation can take many forms, indeed each of us needs to find our own way of creating the space. There are as many ways as there are people.

Many find that repetitive manual work can become so absorbing that they are able to 'loose themselves', and through this process they allow other ideas and inspiration to come in. A simple example would be to set yourself the task of building a wall, not just a small one, but something which will take a while, maybe a few weeks. Then to work on this wall every day for an hour or two, however long is needed to actually forget the every day concerns. Such a task will involve a range of disciplines and skills:- measuring, preparing the ground, foundations, straight or other line work, buying the materials, preparing the tools, mixing the cement, placing the bricks, admiring your work, cleaning your tools. The process allows you to become more receptive to your own creativity, and you build a thing of beauty at the same time, how practical is that! These are the tasks that quieten the voices in your head. By doing this you become more receptive to creativity and inspiration, either during the wall making, or when you then attend to your creative process afterwards, whatever that may be. Some people find their inspiration whilst driving, or running, others whilst washing up or doing the house work. Simple repetitive tasks, which can be boring, dull and uninspiring, are the key to inspiration and creativity (now that's a concept!) If we come at any job or task from the right mental direction it can be a source of joy and delight, rather than a drudge and chore. This is one effect of applying creativity. We are able to transform the mundane into the extraordinary without much effort. Many people find the simple use of meditation or breathing exercises, yoga or other movement patterns, can clear the mind and allow a little gap in our busy minds to form. There is a huge diversity of ways in which we can find a little bit of peace. Some days, we may use a combination of the above. Other days we may be able to just jump straight in, it all depends. The most important part is to recognise that discipline is needed, if you can do it regularly you will change your creative ability and improve, don't beat yourself up if you can't do it every day.

The concept that we are channels for our creativity needs to be explained some more, as it underpins all aspects of creative collaboration. When we have stilled our minds we are able to be in the flow of creativity more easily, we are plugged into a source. This is external to us as individuals. It comes through us, the less baggage in the way the better, and the stronger the flow. As individuals we find this a little offensive to our egos, *"hold on, I'm the one who's being creative, it's my creativity, it's my art work"*. When we think these thoughts and we judge our work or other people's work in this way, we are stopping the creativity. As individuals we are only ever as good as we allow ourselves to be. Our creative work is only ever a reflection of how much faith we have in ourselves, and how much belief we have in the process. I know that as individuals we can develop our skills and abilities, and this is a very important part of the creative collaborative process. But the inspiration for such work is 'through' us, not 'ours alone'.

All creative people need to be able to separate themselves from their art in order to allow better art to come through. Part of the honing and development of our technique involves letting go of expectations and prejudices, and the exploration of a wide range of creative skills. If we comprehend that these skills are coming through us we are able to develop them further, we are not restricted in our use of them. When we allow the creativity to flow we find different solutions to our problems, rather than always following the same path, we explore new ones. For instance, a painter may always work in oils onto canvas. Over the years this leads to a specialisation that creates excellence in terms of techniques, which can lead to fame and fortune. However, if as part of that artist's creative practice they were to do some water-colour painting, write a little poetry, or some dance as well, they will find that their oil painting will improve at the same time. I'm not suggested that they water down their work, I am suggesting that they need to be in a constant dialogue with their creativity in order for it to be able to grown and change. I believe creativity needs to be diverse and changing. The creation of specialisations can only lead to stagnation and a lack of inspiration at the end. Creative collaboration can lead to good art, we will create great art if we let go of our fears and doubts, there is no alternative!

For me, we are all in 'debt' to our creativity. We use it every day if we are artists. We have created industries from it. We are able to feed and nourish our families from its' fruits, but we don't honour it and respect it in the way in which we should. As individuals we all have talents and abilities which mark us out from others, we need to work with these in two ways:-

- *Develop them, improve them and strive to use them for the benefit of others*
- *Nurture our abilities, give thanks for them, and know that we owe them a debt of gratitude and thanks*

If we don't do this we stagnate, we become moribund, we fill with ego, we believe that we are important, we miss out on lots of further opportunities for growth and strength. So, the honouring of our creativity is the next major task we must undertake if we are to become a good channel, we need to pay our respects. This can be through the creation of art works that are not for sale, which are not for public consumption. A sculptor can create a work of art that is not seen by anyone else. This is to be as good as any of the other artworks made, indeed, it could be the best one ever. The work is then left in either a secret or wild place. Or a singer could sing their work in a wild place, not to an audience, and never perform it in front of people. By doing so you are honouring your abilities, the creativity which flows through you. You are showing that you realize creativity is beyond money, beyond materialism and greed, it is about beauty. You enable beauty to become manifest in the world. You need to understand that by creating art you have used up valuable materials, you have used the earth's resources, you have manifested a physical presence (even as a song). You need to pay your debts and you do this by creating beauty that is specifically for the earth, for the planet, which is not about ego and not about yourself. By doing this on a regular basis you will increase your creative abilities. You will be blessed by increased creativity, you will ensure that you remember how important the task of manifesting beauty is. I know people may not believe this, but I know it to be true, and I know a lot of other people who have worked this way and found the benefits.

We also need to relate this creative process to the collaborative nature of humanity - appreciating the ways in which we can manifest beauty with others. As 'community art' and 'art in the community' have developed over the past 30 years many have stepped away from making individual art, and concentrated on making collaborative work. This has been very beneficial to all concerned, thousands of people have grown stronger from this sharing. However some of those community arts practitioners have lost touch with their own creative sparks (I include myself as one). We became so absorbed in the creation of collaborative art works we no longer created our own. This can become debilitating as well, it's a question of balance, and it's also a question of what is appropriate. When I was young and just starting out, I needed to focus all my attention on raising the profile of community art, and ensuring that my friends were employed full time. So necessarily, my own creativity waned, I did use my creativity to provide the jobs for others. However now I am more experienced, no longer in my twenties (thankfully!) I have a good range of projects, I can pick and choose from them. I can spend more time on my own creativity. This is a vital component in the development of a good professional community artist.

The ability to 'breath', to rest and recuperate, to restore yourself. A community artist is giving most of the time. By 'giving' I mean working to generate an environment conducive to growth for others, but you also need to grow yourself. If you are a professional community artist who believes in creative collaboration you will strive to improve yourself and the work you create with others, so you need to take time out and restore yourself. Take time to do your own personal work, or by experimenting in new techniques.

Community artists can not afford to stand still, they need to be in perpetual motion. There is no room for stagnation, for complacency and working to a formula. Every project must be better than the last, every project must be a challenge to you and those participating. Only you know when you are doing this and when you aren't. The best way of ensuring that this occurs is to have change as an integral part of the process. Change will ensure that growth occurs, the change can be in the types of art work you do, the groups you do it with, or the other artists you work with.

When we work in creativity we are working passionately, we are actually being consumed by inspiration, life, vitality and joy. This is a very exciting process, but it can also lead to burn out and decay. Passion is hot. It needs to be handled with understanding otherwise it can eat you up, drag you away, and when it has finished with you, you become embittered and cynical. So, be careful, and ensure that you take time for yourself, think of your needs, before you become either too tired or too bitter. The capacity to change and adapt, the ability to breath and rest, these are the personal skills we need to learn alongside our creative abilities, we need to apply our creativity at all moments of the day, as well as living a balanced and sensible life.

Many artists become specialists, they focus, and they pursue dreams or ideals that lead to a very small world-view.

This can be damaging for yourself and for those around you, although the present Western culture does tend to encourage and reward such behaviour. As creative people we have a responsibility to apply our creativity to a wide range of tasks, courses and situations. The very potency of our visioning abilities make us ideal catalysts for change, both on a small and large scale. So, don't shine your light in just one direction, be adventurous, daring and expansive, it's time to change. Artists need to collaborate and seek visions within their own fields, and then outwards into ecology, science, physics, mathematics, any number of subjects. Get radical.

Chapter Eleven
Work with others

Through my college years we were encouraged to pursue an individual path and create work on our own. This is a necessary stage in evolving your creative identity, it enables us to develop our creative skills. We were not encouraged to collaborate and missed opportunities to pool resources, or experience the power of a 'group' project. Individuals do indeed create works which come through their imagination and which touch everyone's hearts and souls. However, even these lone wolves are actually working collaboratively. There is always a relationship to an audience. Unless you are independently able to support yourself, there is a need to earn a living by your skill. Also, there is a need for peer feedback, we need to be able to have at least one person with whom we can discuss our art and our thoughts. This is part of the human condition, and those that say they don't need it are in denial.

The development of an individual creative process, be that in dance, drama, voice work, film, the visual arts, whatever, will always be influenced by others. We are influenced by our peers, by those we love, by those we hate. We are influenced by others outside our immediate field - inspired by artists from the past, by images on film or television. We will be influenced by the culture in which we live at the moment, and by our perceptions of past cultures. If our work is for a specific audience then their tastes and views will change the way we work. If we are funded by particular bodies then we will adapt our work to suit their needs, however much we don't think we do! The creative process is always being influenced by others, we need to be able to include this in our work process, and to ensure that we are aware of how we are being influenced.

As individual artists we are always creating and establishing support structures, and these are the strongest, most potent, influences on our work. Often we do this unconsciously, indeed, it is human nature to work this way. I believe all creative people need to gain as wide a range of such influences as possible, and they can take many forms.

Peer group Who do you trust and respect amongst the people you know? The answer may come as a surprise, in that sometimes the people whose opinions we need to seek are not obviously connected to your creative activities. That's fine, you need to identify people you trust and to use them as barometers in terms of your work, ask their opinions, seek their advice. This needs to be done on a regular basis, because we can often become so enmeshed in our own struggles that we don't notice how time flies, how small we have become, how intransigent our motives. It is a great compliment to be asked your opinion by someone else, so those chosen should respond well, but be careful in whom you choose, and obviously be flexible and change these people over time.

Mentors As an extension of this support structure, we all need mentors. People, who have more experience, people who know what they are doing, people to aspire to. Culturally we are told this is very important in your teens and twenties, which it is, but actually we need them throughout our lives. It is important that a creative person aspires to develop their work, and mentors can enable you to do this. They can be people you've heard of, people you've come across, and thought, *"Wow, they've really got their act together".* To develop a relationship with a mentor is very important, it is a complex relationship which I don't have the time to fully explain here, but I can give some pointers.

In my own life for quite a time during my twenties I was firmly convinced that no one could teach me anything. I was a pioneer in the true sense of the word, and I was unique. This meant I was also a bit cynical, a bit arrogant and very opinionated! In my early thirties I had quite a number of problems which I found very hard to deal with, and co-incidentally the chance to contact someone I had know about ten years previously. He was ten years older than me and was able to say *"Yes, I know what you're dealing with, this is what you need to do."* Part of me instantly rejected his advice, but gradually I realised that he was telling the truth. He did know what I was going through. I was not unique. He was able to help me through a very difficult patch, by showing me how my experiences were common to a lot of people, a great teaching. At the same time I had always thought of him as being very sorted and very aware. Through having a closer relationship I was able to see his frailties and his vulnerabilities. This was a great blessing for me, as it encouraged me to be more vulnerable and open. Having a mentor is not about having someone who is always right, it is about being able to confide in someone, and being encouraged to grow, through being admired and respected. A good mentor will let you grow, not try to teach you doctrines or brain wash you, but just admire and encourage you.

This is a very important principle, the concept of mutual support. We are not particularly aware of it in the West, and we need to bring it into our work practice and lives. If we support others, we encourage them, we praise them - we are positive - they and others will in turn do the same to us. If we don't support others, if we are cynical- we don't believe - they and others will do the same to us. There is reciprocity in mutual support that needs to be acknowledged and worked with. As a generalisation, those active in the arts tend to have not done well academically. How this has come about is a very interesting area, I would suggest it's something like this.

In general terms most schools are pretty dull, academic and 'mind' orientated places, where you can get by if you use the left side of your brain. If, however, you are using mainly the right side of your brain - your intuition and creativity - you are bound to find it hard to succeed in school. You are a creative type, someone who thinks differently. The subjects you are likely to succeed in are art or drama, something creative, indeed you will have found solace there. On the whole the other subjects will have been boring and difficult to follow. This may have led to a tendency to be bored during these other lessons, which can lead to trouble. Therefore, you will have tended to have been chastised, criticised and made an example of in school. School will have taught you some bad habits, and you will need to be praised and encouraged, following this bad experience. Coming from this background, you need to be supported through your career in terms of being praised, encouraged and being told that you are good. So, surround yourself with positive people. Indeed, if you want to change the way our culture is going, you need to be part of a movement to encourage mutual support. To stop the way in which many of us were and continue to be brought up in schools and other institutions. Teachers need to understand that they are very powerful influences, and simply by being positive and supportive, they can bring about tremendous change. There are many teachers who know this and act upon it, they are the ones we all remember and are thankful to. These teachers are the way for the future, not the ones who cling to the idea that children need a return to discipline and the way things were in Victorian times.

Support Groups Artists are able to form groups, we can do this either loosely and informally as and when the need arises, just don't be afraid of doing it! We can develop this formally to create businesses and companies, or informally as friends or mutual assistants. Either way, I believe, can be very helpful to you as an individual practitioner. It will stimulate a diversity of changes both within your work, the services you offer, and eventually the way in which you earn your living. I, personally, formed a group, which started very informally, but then we went through classic transformations. From being a loose collective of self employed people; into a co-operative; to a limited company and people becoming paid full time; and then finally into a not for profit company (almost charitable status). These transformations happened over a 20-year period, and obviously reflect the levels of seriousness of the participating artists. My only advice is.....don't go rushing into anything. There is always time to become serious. At certain points in my life I have been a Director of up 5 different companies, but now I am back and happy as being a sole trader, you never can tell! In addition, don't get too close, any group or team will move on. If a group you have started is stagnating, do something about it, or get out, be loose and adaptable.

Network A key part of this process is to ensure that we are networking with others. One of the most frequently heard complaints from artists and creative people is how alone and unsupported they feel. When we are being mutually supportive to others, we will be supported by others. Information will always pass two ways. By having regular meetings with other people, by forming small informal groups you are ensuring that the information about yourself is up to date and of value. All too often, I come across people who say "*Oh, I know you, you do mosaics*" I haven't made a mosaic in three years. It's not their fault, it just shows how we are easily compartmentalised, and If we don't keep people informed of changes, they won't know. As a group this is a lot easier to maintain, but as individuals we need to be aware of how important this is. Most jobs in the creative industries are gained through word of mouth and personal recommendations, we are almost entirely as good as our last job. We create a reputation and this is based on our recent past.

However, you can restrict yourself by only offering the things you know you can do. Perhaps you have other untapped resources and skills to offer? For me there was a point at which I left The Pioneers and had to re-invent myself, because I wanted to work more with men and boys, rather than just school children. It took about 6 months for me to gain my first job in that new direction, and I was constantly being offered jobs I had out-grown. I had to risk making a fool of myself to get this new work, but it has definitely been worthwhile.

Keep people informed in whatever ways are easy for you, you can keep this process changing and moving forward, through the internet, whatever. Community art is at present changing rapidly, this is a new career path. It didn't exist 20 years ago, so don't be trapped and confined by funding bodies and present ideologies. For me, community art and it's transmogrification into creative collaboration has to seek alternatives which are challenging. This may mean exploring LETS schemes, supporting fair pay for work, not exploiting people or materials. We have to join in at the cutting edge of our culture. Just because we are now receiving the kind of recognition we deserved a long time ago, doesn't mean we all have to put on suits and become the establishment.

If you do form a group, then be imaginative about whom you form it with. Why not people from other arts disciplines? I'm all in favour of cross-art fertilization. You can also form alliances with people from outside the arts, community development, ecological and sustainable issues, why restrict yourselves? This will then lead to a broader range of new and innovative projects being offered. Projects which are presently outside the funding remits of the Arts Council need to be started now! When I first went to the Arts Council and said I wanted to work in a school to paint a mural, they said they couldn't fund it, as it didn't fit into any of their criteria. Can you imagine that nowadays! This has always been a vital area for me. Don't be funding led, try to keep to innovative and imaginative schemes. Nowadays it is common place for artists to be involved in residencies, training schemes, workshops, exhibitions and performances by community groups, mentoring schemes, all of these were very sparse on the ground just 20 years ago. So, go for it, and create the innovative and exciting projects for the next 20 years.

Chapter Twelve

Work in the wider community

The way in which we behave will affect how we work with others. It is only through undertaking this journey of understanding ourselves, setting up support structures and exploring what we can offer the world, that we finally reach the goal of working with our communities. In the first chapters I took quite a long look at community and how we relate to it. Here I want to just ask you to be as imaginative as possible ,and to look at how progressive we, as artists, can become. Most of western civilization is based on a premise that everyone and everything is compartmentalised, this is supposed to make our lives easier. However, it does have a tendency to weaken the individual and to ensure that corporations and specialists are kept in business.

I want to ask one key question of anyone who wants to be an artist, do you want to perpetuate the present exploitative nature of our culture? If the answer is "*yes*", then fine, carry on, but you aren't going to agree with the essence of this book. If the answer is "*no*", then let's work together to find new ways. The trouble is those new ways don't exist yet, and there are mortgages to be paid in the meantime. I know and appreciate this, but I still believe it is our duty to seek to change what is presently a very out of balance culture and move towards ideals and goals we can only dream about.

In the 1960's and '70's when community art was in it's infancy, we were part of a movement which felt the revolution was imminent. We believed the 'establishment' had let us down, and there were basic inequalities in our society which were unfair and unjust. My position hasn't changed, the inequality is still there, possibly worse, but I have been absorbed into the 'establishment' (that's such an old fashioned word, but I love it). It is important to re-examine exactly what we set out to do, and see if we have been diverted. I wanted to set up some alternatives to the way in which the world was organised, to make art which addressed the basic inequality of our culture. I think I have failed in that. Indeed, there is a strong argument saying community artists were mostly employed on the back of the riots of the early 1980's to appease and placate the working classes. We made their lives just tolerable enough to stop them rioting. Then we were part of an assimilation programme that encouraged them to stay in their place. I know a lot of dedicated community artists will object to this analysis, but it is my place to question myself and my own motivations. If I upset others I am sorry, but I'm not doing this out of spite or remorse. I still burn brightly, indeed the older I get the more radical I become. I am angry about social injustice and deprivation, and I know that creativity can be used to overcome and change such situations.

Interestingly our language has been subtly altered, we are now involved in community development, social inclusion, regeneration - before we were fighting inequality, poverty and injustice. Let's rediscover our passion, we can do that collaboratively, and then we'll really see what we can do. The older generation of community artists, which I represent, need to find ways of passing on their experience in a way that is not dictatorial. I don't know what is best, but I can encourage the next generation to explore and discover better and more relevant ways. In a sense The Pioneers was an example of artists working collaboratively in a new way. We didn't employ administrators, we worked as one whole, doing the admin and the projects. We actually incorporated aspects of collaboration, mutual support and creativity into the artistic venture. Nowadays, such a structure is seen as impractical because of the sheer volume and scale of administration, evaluation and compromise needed to be a publicly accountable company. What I am seeking from the next generation of artists is a challenge to that premise. Challenge why we should all be accountable, who we should be accountable to. Why we need so many specialists, so many middlemen and women. My art and creativity is not about men in suits, it is about spirit, setting people free, belief in the power of the imagination. Let's get back there, let's get angry, let's get into our emotions, let's not hold back!

In a sense I have written myself out of a book here, the future form and shape of creative collaboration is unseen right now, I can't prejudge it, and I shouldn't try to push it in any particular direction. The future shape of community art needs to come from the creation of collaborations. Ideas that make me scared because I've not worked that way before. Recently, I was asked to start a series of workshops for youth and community workers. This was new work for me, creating a series of projects that look at the very distinct way in which men behave. How they teach, how they communicate, and how to encourage them to be mutually supportive. Such work scares me, I am stepping into places I've never worked before. I know that such work is the only way forward. I'm not the only one working this way, the impact of this will have long-term effects on me, other artists and the people we are working with.

I am presuming that those of you reading this are similar to me, you burn with passion, and this is precious beyond all theory and experience. This internal fire needs to believe in creativity, and the value of being creative to society as a whole. Allied to this there is a need for a burning belief in the injustice of the world, as well as a desire to change yourself and others for the better. Many people don't know what it is they want from life. They fall into things, they amble around until something fires them up. That's fine, I certainly didn't know I was going to be a community artist all my life until after several years of being one. I didn't know at 21 what I wanted to be. I still don't. I collaborated and created opportunities which didn't exist at that time. My motivation certainly wasn't money, my motivation wasn't connected with the long term, I just did it.

However, in the background of this was a fire, a desire, to make a difference. Every artist needs to contact their internal fire through whatever means they have and to follow that. Find the things which make you happy, the things you believe in, combine them, and make a job out of it…it sounds so simple! For many this is a very difficult journey, they have been suppressed, many don't even know they have an internal fire. It was only by being bold, only by making mistakes, by being frustrated, by being humiliated, that I found what I was truly about. Sometimes, it is only in adversity that we find who we are. There is the paradox of passion, only by making mistakes can you start to see what is good work, what is driving you, and what is just treading water. When an artist is really being creative you start to take risks, you start to challenge yourself, and this is a vital componant in an artists skill pack. I acknowledge that sometimes the mistakes we make can be very painful, they can restrict us, but I know that as individuals we need to accept sometimes we are going to not quite do as well as we thought. Those moments can be great teachers. I believe it is essential that creative people realise that by making themselves vulnerable, by taking risks, they can strengthen themselves. When you make a mistake, please learn from it, ask for help, ask for support, it will come. Follow your instincts, make things happen, get out there in your communities and start making art. Start collaborating, offering yourself as a resource, as a catalyst for change. You will be surprised by the diversity of support and interest there are out there for your ideas and beliefs. I have always been surprised by the support I have received, from the most unlikely sources, from accountants, engineers, bank managers, planning officers, local government officials, they all enjoy creativity.

So, are there any useful tips I can pass on in terms of how to do the work? Yes, a few, I'll try to keep them simple and clear. Most of all I want to enable creative people from all disciplines to understand them, so they will be basic. I don't want to have a big section in the book about how to organise your sessions, who to work with, health and safety, cultural diversity, or any other such subject. There are plenty of helpful books and information about setting up workshops. In a sense that is all subjective, each workshop is different, each group we work with is a new challenge. We can work with the same group for a morning, then the afternoon, and the dynamic can be totally different. To set down hard and fast rules is impossible. All I can give are some guidelines in terms of what you are doing and how this should progress.

I think there is a progression involved in creative collaboration. A great deal depends on the qualities that you the artist bring to the work - you need to be open, (outwardly) confident and willing to adapt and change. A basic principle in any workshop is always to be two steps ahead of your participants. If they are doing an arts activity, you need to know not only what they can do next, but also where that leads. So, for instance, if they are making a basic mosaic, you need to know what kind of questions they will ask next - *"how do I cut the corners off to make a circle?"* and where such a question will lead *"I want to make this look more realistic."* But, before we step into those areas, I need to just remind you of what we are all involved in. As a community artist I have made mosaics, large scale painting, stained glass windows, videos, photography projects, storytelling, whatever, and for me there is no fear involved in those processes. For most of the people I have worked with such activities are alien. They have no previous experience of it, and this can be very intimidating. So, in order to ease people into such activities I use 'gateways' to the actual making or doing. If I were to undertake a drawing project with a group of people who had never drawn before, and I placed a blank sheet of paper with a pencil in front of them and said *"draw",* many will be intimidated and many will not draw. I need to ease them into drawing, I need to make the process simple, attractive and enjoyable. I may start with simple doodling and movement exercises. I talk about how hard or not hard to grip the pencil, I talk about the line produced in terms of thickness, lightness of touch. I just give them lots of information in a humorous and light way. We all start using the paper and pencils collaboratively. Exploring what we can do, and then by magic, we are all drawing! This applies to all kinds of art - dance, drama, movement - they are all wonderful tools to draw people into arts activities. You need to use a simple 'gateway' of fun, explanation, relaxation, getting out of the mental into the physical, and then you can start the serious work. It's like the exercises I talked about in Chapter Ten which relate to your own practice, you need to lead people lightly and gently to the work, not heavy handedly.

If we are armed with this consciousness, then really the workshops can develop easily, normally along the following lines:-

∑ *from initial contacts, being friendly, supportive and informal*
∑ *winning trust through close contact, personal work and praise*
∑ *developing new skills, challenging personal ideas and previously held attitudes*
∑ *creating collaborative works which mutually support*
∑ *passing on skills and techniques*
∑ *creating pride, ownership and personal development*

I remember speaking with a good landscape painter who expressed her surprise at the fact that often during her classes people would suddenly burst into tears whilst painting. She felt uncomfortable and embarrassed about it. I felt the opposite, it showed me how well she was working! Creativity, despite being undertaken in a collaborative process, in a workshop, amongst friends or strangers, is an intensely personal experience. When anyone is involved in that process it will be operating on a number of levels within their physical and mental bodies, let alone their spiritual and other bodies.

Creativity unlocks past traumas, can develop our awareness of ourselves immensely. That is why it is such a potent tool, why this work must be done. Artists who facilitate these processes must be aware of this, and must always be supportive and able to empathize. I'll develop this more later. To return to the participants, there is normally a mental process involved in such activities and it relates directly to their levels of self-awareness and confidence. It can be summed up in three phrases, which I hear all the time:-

"I can't do that"

"Let me have a go"

"How can I improve what I've done"

Those phrases sum up a good community arts workshop, they are the levels of expectation that the participants normally have for themselves, and they reflect a progression all community artists need to strive towards. If at the end of the session or process people are being critical of their own work, you are winning. This means they have set themselves a goal and surpassed it. We can not ask for more, and this state of mind is the ideal fertile ground into which a variety of seeds can planted:-

"You are good at this"

"You've made a piece of art"

"You could take this a lot further"

This is the stage at which you can introduce the principles of being two steps ahead, you no longer need to work with disguised 'gateways'. The individuals will be all creating their own 'gateways' and expectations. They will be expecting to improve, and in this moment we have create a change in the way in which they are behaving and reacting. The artist therefore becomes a 'role model', and this is the next stage of developing the relationship with the participant. You will need to assume a range of responsibilities and concerns for their work, which until this point have not been there. This process can take weeks or years with some people, it can take hours with others, or minutes, you never know! As the role model you encourage and support the participants - you know where they could go and how to enable them to get there. In addition you need to be unstinting with your praise and encouragement. This is not the soft option.

Many artists who start working with community groups don't expect much from their participants so they say *"Oh, that's lovely, well done"*, when they are thinking *"Gawd, that's a poor piece of work"*. This is dishonest and the participants know themselves their work is not good enough. It's a fine line to tread. You don't need to be brutal, that will just discourage, but you must encourage progress and movement at all times. This will lead to ownership and pride, and that is the whole principle of community arts activities in all their shapes and forms. This element is lacking in some artists' practice - they think they need to put themselves up as the teacher - equated with knowing all the answers. This is wrong, the role model is just two steps ahead most of the time, doesn't know all the answers, and can be vulnerable, uncertain and human. Indeed, good role models never forget to learn at all times. They show how they are learning too, how they continue to learn and how they are grateful to their pupils for teaching them. Remember community art, creative collaboration, call it what you may, is a new way of being, not a perpetuation of the present education system.

Role models are also experimenting with new techniques, trying things out, welcoming change. This can have a very powerful effect on your participants. The knock on effects of being like this are immense and not to be discounted. You may well influence people into changing their jobs, or changing their patterns of behaviour, just by being yourself. I went through a creative process with a group of 12 youth and community workers for a weekend, and within a month three had left their job!

This is the key to the next stage of development in such work, by being supportive you have enabled the individuals to work collaboratively and creatively. This will now affect their self-view, their self worth, their whole demeanour. From working on a, for want of a better word, superficial level, you are now deepening the experience. The individuals will start to explore a concept of 'identity'. This invariably happens. It is the consequence of such work. Individuals start to create their own identities, start to explore group identities. Creative collaboration will always come down to who we are and where we come from, and when it is working well, where we are going. You can work with any group of people, of any ability, of any age, and at the end of the process, you will always end up with work reflecting the personalities involved and exploring their identity.

Chapter Thirteen
"Do you get paid to do this?"

The amount of times I have been asked this question, I'm sat on the floor with twenty children studiously making a huge painted banner. The look of astonishment on people's faces when I say:
"Yes. Not only do I get paid to do this but I also employ four other people and we work all over the world and have done for the last 20 years."

Why should this be such a remarkable statement? Why should this be so amazing? Something is fundamentally wrong with a culture that can't imagine such work should be paid for. There is now a grudging acknowledgement of the worth of the arts, we've almost caught up with sport in terms of public awareness of being *'a good thing'*. But, to actually gain employment on a full time basis, and to earn good money, that is not registering yet. So, the next stage for creative collaborators is to convince the wider community that not only is it a good thing, but it needs to be paid well and respected. The roots of this lack of respect are traced in the first chapters, so I don't want to go over that ground again. Suffice to say, we are seen as a luxury, as an add-on, not essential. The majority of artists add to this problem rather than fight it. Many creative people have real difficulties saying how much they want to be paid, let alone actually going out and getting it. The separation of money from creativity is imbued in artists, and the culture in which we live continues to perpetuate these myths. My father would greet me with the same question for many years *"Have you got a proper job yet?"* Despite the fact that I was actually earning enough to support my young family. This problem is reflected in the history of community arts, we were all volunteers when we started, there was no job called 'community artist'. The practice has become professionalised, but the rest of society keeps us in the place of volunteering.

The great majority of community arts organisations have been reliant on Arts Council and Local Authority subsidy to survive. This is fine, I can't think of a better way of spending public money, but it has created a reliance on funding which is always dangerous. As a subsidised industry we are vulnerable to rapid decreases as a result of political whims and fancies, and how much we are able to play the political games. The recent decline in Lottery funding, due to people no longer wanting to buy into it, has also exposed us. This is not a safe or secure place to be. Where the community arts movement can turn to seek funding which can be called secure is problematic. In a sense, there is a paradox here, community arts activities are high risk, and when they become safe and secure they loose some of their impact. However, I would suggest we need to seek an imaginative and creative approach to the problem. The core values which we need to promote are:

- *community artists need to be paid a decent living wage which equates to the value of their work. We are professionals/consultants/administrators/managers/ teachers - who facilitate radical change within people*
- *community art needs to be an integrated part of an overall strategy for the long term health and welfare of our society*

For too long we have been underpaid and undervalued. Expected to do long hours in squalid conditions for the love of it. In addition we have been perceived as the luxury, the add-on, not the real content in terms of social change and community development. This has often been self-perpetuated, but the movement as a whole now needs to professionalise and become the sum of its parts. This professionalisation of the practice has started, some of us are now starting to be paid well for the work, but there is still a long way to go in terms of gaining public support. The work we do is a vital link in the development of healthy and enriched individuals- we assist in the prevention of crime; we create a place for racial harmony; we can break down prejudice; we redirect potentially destructive energy into constructive, creative projects; and so much more. This kind of work is of value and needs to be developed, it isn't a luxury and something you do in your spare time. This whole issue needs to be addressed, and the only way it can be changed is through certain developments:-

- *Community arts organisations need to develop good training and mentoring programmes, as well as a clear model of the new career path which has been created, so it can be understood by the practitioners as well as the funders.*
- *The local authorities, health services, care and probation services, and all the other agencies we work with need to incorporate creativity into their primary provision. Creativity needs to be fundamental to their practice and they need to pay 100% of the costs for such provision, not be subsidised by the Arts Council or Lottery.*
- *The dissemination of information and details of the practice need to be collated, presented and developed as an integral package for local government, government and other institutions. Community art needs to become a pressure group for it's own good, thus far we have just done the work and expected people to know about it, that is not good enough.*

At present there is stagnation in the public funding for all arts activities which does not bode well for the future. The Arts Council has a number of revenue clients that increasingly eat up more and more of the budget as their income declines. This is true in both the high arts and community arts fields. Community arts must separate itself from this process to show the way forward. In order for our movement to be truly radical and progressive we need to undertake new ways of being, and to show how to do this to the establishment. I would suggest that established community arts organisations need to ensure that the percentage of funding coming from new sources - such as direct from health authorities, the clients you are working for - increases so that you can decrease dependence on the Arts Council. This will free up funding in the Arts Council for new community arts organisations, who will in turn develop new ways of working and existing. There is a motion, a rhythm, to this kind of work, it starts with innovation and new ideas, these lead to revenue status and establishment of professionalism, which needs to lead to a stimulation of new growth and innovation. This cycle is essential to ensure change and growth, right now the Arts Council is stagnating and has lost its' rhythm. We need to ensure that the long term is being considered in the short term.

Crucial to this is the forming of new alliances with partners beyond the existing range of contacts. Community artists, creative collaborators, need to be imaginative and progressive in their work, and we can form alliances with the ecological, sustainable, spiritual, health promoting organisations. We can form alliances and joint funding packages with woodland developments, with organic growers, with alternative technological centres, with engineers and with scientists. We need to apply our creativity in ways we have never thought of before, and create projects we have just dreamed about. If we don't, we will become bogged down in the bureaucratic mess which surround work in the present education system, the arts establishment and our cultural industry. We can still work in these fields, but we need to become radical voices for change, we need to stir up the stagnant waters, bring fresh ideas and new concepts. The movement needs to look at the development of businesses for community benefit, at the creation of locally sustainable initiatives that meet a very specific need, create employment and new visions.

These alliances already exist. Most practicing community artists have many strings to their bows, that's how we have all survived. We are intelligent and inquisitive individuals who want to learn and diversify, we just haven't quite understood how far we have come. Presently we are working in a limited and restricted area, community art. We have many contacts beyond this area, but we are not using them, or we lack the confidence to bring them into our 'work'. I'll give an example, I was at a major community arts conference in Amsterdam in the early 1990's. Serious artists, real heroes of mine, lots of booze, lots of talk, but cautious, because we'd never really all sat round a table before. We'd gone through art and creativity and were now into alternative therapies, spirituality and other such stuff. One very brave soul said *"As community artists we've all been healers, that really is the work we do, and we need to recognise it and bring it into our work."* After the initial shocked silence we slowly admitted that we had all been doing various things like that *"I'm learning to be an osteopath", "I'm doing ritual and ceremony".* We realised we had all been involved in a wide range of activities which we had separated from our arts practice, from the way in which we 'earn a living'. Also, we realised that the creative process in itself is a healing process, and why we are drawn to such a diversity of other skills and practices. The more holistic we are in terms of bringing all the different aspects of ourselves to the work, the better it is for the people we work with, the broader and more expansive the work will become. New ways of working will be created, not by hiding our interests and beliefs, not by separating ourselves into component parts, but by integrating all aspects of our lives into becoming the way we are and the way in which we earn our money.

Your interests and hobbies are the new way of earning money in the near future. As creative people we need to grasp this concept, work to our full potential, and make sure that we are not limiting ourselves. If we believe that the present culture is fundamentally flawed and wrong we can withdraw from it, and try to live outside it (although this is impossible in Britain right now), or we can challenge it and show alternatives. One way in which we show alternatives is through our passion, through our enthusiasm and belief in beauty. Right now there are very few people who are in touch with their passion, there are very few people who live this way. Creative collaborators, community artists, need to show others how to do this. I believe it is an artists' duty and responsibility to use their innate creativity. By doing so we create the employment opportunities for the next generation, we become social entrepreneurs.

Interestingly, in recent years within the field of psychology there has been research into the links between creativity and enterprise, mainly looking at how individuals identified as entrepreneurs, differ from the rest of society. The research shows most entrepreneurs have applied their own innate creativity to ordinary situations to come up with an extraordinary solution. This shows a great deal of similarity between artists' thought patterns and entrepreneurs. So, please don't hold back on those wildly imaginative ideas, they are just as valid as anyone elses!

Chapter Fourteen
It gets under your skin and is all over the place

To be involved in creativity is to open oneself to strong emotions and feelings, which can take you by surprise. This shows the strong link between creativity and self-awareness. Every person involved in creative work is exploring their own ideas, and, by the nature of the practice, they are being enriched, growing. When we grow, we increase our self-awareness and knowledge. A direct result of increased awareness is increased inquisitiveness and boosted confidence. Children tend to ask more questions, tend to have a clearer idea of the world and their relationship to it, after their creativity has been stimulated.

Unbelievably, this can be seen as a problem, often teachers find a class has become very lively after they have worked with the arts, and some find that difficult. An extreme example of this was during a video project we ran in Swansea. A group of comprehensive school children worked with us for a week to make adverts, using professional equipment, and really enjoyed the opportunity. On the last day one of their mums came storming in and ranted *"You've made my life a misery, Sharon comes home now and she won't shut up, she talks all the way through the programmes I want to watch. 'Look at that camera angle, do you know why they did that?' I just want her to shut up."* Instead of rejoicing in her daughter's newfound interest she wanted a return to the passive acceptance of ignorance.

We tended to create huge works of art, this meant we ensured the participants worked collaboratively, they had to in order to finish the work. Team building, awareness of personal and group responsibilities, are all very important life skills which are intuitively gained through this work. In addition the group are able to identify themselves, not only just about what they have done, but what they have achieved, and where they come from. So many of societies' present problems stem from individuals not having a positive identity or a value to others. Linked to this is another very important issue, respect. The individuals achieved something on a scale and to a finish they didn't initially expect. This increased their own pride and sense of achievement, it also affects other people's attitude to them, teachers, parents, grandparents see them in a different light. This is of huge benefit to our society as a whole. I could go on, further and deeper, but I hope you've got the picture.

So, to briefly summarize the effects expected of a community arts project with children: -

Short term effects of community art

∑ *It provides employment for community artists*

∑ *It will change the child's/participants outlook about art and artists*

∑ *It will give them a sense of pride in their achievement*

∑ *It will help them understand what it is to work in a team*

∑ *It can possibly overcome some early prejudices and fears*

∑ *It will improve the teachers/youth/care workers relationship to their children/youths/adults through mutual admiration and respect*

∑ *It will improve the status of young people in their community as news of their achievement spreads*

∑ *It will change their relationship with their parents, other adults in their community*

Long term effects

∑ *It can lead to their gaining better and more worthwhile or fulfilling jobs in the future*

∑ *It can lead to a reduction in criminal activity*

∑ *It can lead to better relationships between generations in their community*

This, and so much more, is happening all over Britain, all over Europe right now, it has been going on for many years, I hope it can only increase and improve. Thus far community art has just scratched the surface of what is possible, it has been poorly funded, sidelined and ignored.

I know that a lot of people have never heard of community art, and a lot who have, think it's just keeping children out of trouble, therapy for the masses. There are however many well-established community arts organisations employing hundreds of people all over the world, it's been a silent revolution. In South Wales alone there are at least 12 organisations, they provide over 50 full time workers. In addition there are many individual practitioners creating great projects throughout Britain. This is an industry which is growing and increasing, a positive and encouraging sign for the future.

Chapter Fifteen
Process and Product

"Art is a unique form of experience which can not be imitated in any other way. It is not only non-verbal, it is pre-verbal and since all human beings...gain a large proportion of their experience and understanding through sight and touch, it is very much a part of educational grounding and potential." *ix

I believe when we act creatively we can become self aware. With this awareness we can improve our community and environment, we influence others, and bring about change in the way our society behaves. In order to do this we need to be very flexible and open to ideas. Most artists think of themselves as such, however, an experience on a recent training course shows how far some of us still have to go. Mark Bick and I ran a series of day workshops for some experienced musicians, artists, and craftspeople. One of the principles we tested was to challenge all of them about their own creativity. We asked them to sing or do another creative activity with each session. Some became so frightened they had to leave the room, others visibly quaked. Each session we asked them to participate in a very simple exercise – dance, draw, etc. - and each session it pressed buttons, brought up fear. Even those who think of themselves as being creative, actually aren't fully reaching their potential. We can all sing, dance, make music, draw, create poetry. Unfortunately, we have been told by others, or ourselves, that we can't do one or some of these things. This book is about a theory that can open up this range of creativity in all of us, and enable us to use it to become whole human beings. Before we can do this, we need to understand that a lot of creativity is being wasted, ignored and marginalised. The majority of people are alienated by art, because they can't believe they have it inside themselves.

Too often community art has been ignored or belittled, mainly because it is actually multi-layered. It is not a simple technique you can master in an afternoon, it needs time and commitment, it is a transformative and growing process. You can work superficially with children, you can allow partial participation. You can skim the surface of something and call yourself an expert, don't we all know people who have done that!

There are many differences between artists and community artists. Good community artists are consummately professional at seeming to be informal and allowing things to grown organically. There was a raging argument in the 1970's and 80's - which is the most important 'process' or 'product'? Process is the way in which you work with the community, how much leeway you allow them in the decision making process, the art creation. Whereas the product is the end result. Is it 'good art' or does it 'look like a bit of therapy". Many artists hide behind a strange argument to justify their poor community art in the following way. *"My individual art is wonderful, strong, emotive, but the work I make with the children is just fun, it's a way of earning some money for me, so the process is all, the product doesn't matter."* This is just not good enough, and it misses the point. Good community art is about process and product, both are important. In some projects the process will dictate the product, but not always. Participants in any project will be making qualitative judgements about the end result, and if they haven't really been challenged in the process then the result will reflect their discontent. A community artist knows this, and devises ways of getting the participants to develop their skills, to challenge themselves, to surprise themselves and others with the results and will also be creating projects which last the test of time. Projects which people can recognise, identify with, can be at home with, and are seen as a positive change.

That is where the joy lies for a community artist - to create wonderful, beautiful art with people who may have never danced, sung, painted, made music or made a mosaic before. It also lies in the collaborative process of working with other artists, other creative people, and in surprising people with the end results. Despite all the prejudices the general public have about 'modern art' they will all have opinions in terms of what is good and bad art. This brings us on to the *'gobsmack factor'*.

When confronted by wonderful creativity – be that a painting, sculpture, piece of music or drama – we react with awe, with respect and with wonder. Good community art has that effect on people, they just can't believe that a bunch of kids made it, or they say, *"I never thought I could do something like that"*. Not all community art is like this, a great many projects are just average, but on occasions there will be projects which elevate themselves above the ordinary, which produce a *'gobsmack'* effect in those that are participating or/ and those viewing. To be part of such a process and product is to be validated, validated as a human being who has tried and succeeded for a little while in doing something of value. Not many people who call themselves artists can claim to have done that.

Community art deals with peoples lives, deals with the real world. Artists need training, lots of it, in order to become good community artists. When we collaborate we become aware of the implications of creativity on the society around us, and this social concern becomes part of the art work, as described in the document **"Arts and Communities"**. ***"Social concern is present in every artist but in art in the community it is fundamental....In the last twenty years the relationship of the arts to communities has been pursued in a variety of ways: extending the reach***

of traditional arts to a wider social spectrum; helping people in particular communities to develop their own arts skills and forms of expression; giving greater recognition to the arts of particular ethnic, cultural, social or occupational groups; and developing critiques of traditional avant-garde or popular arts."*x

Creativity used in the spirit of collaboration, leads to profound change. The community arts in Britain have now become a very professional and well respected industry. This has come about in a very quiet and respectful way. I am so pleased to have been a part of such a movement, and I believe it stands as a direct challenge to the more established high art ways. ***"Certain fine art practices and high arts are protected from the yardstick which is used to measure more socially engaged arts. It has been easy for art world supremacists to dismiss whole areas of practice as 'social art' – seen as decoration, community work, art therapy or play. That it is not considered equal to those other 'proper' art forms which cater to a minority of tastes and to which the majority of funding goes deflects any challenges to the mainstream."*xi***

The community arts movement needs to believe in itself, needs to understand just how powerful it has become, and can become in the future. All human beings are restricted by fear, by anxieties that have been imposed by others, our ancestors, our parents, whoever. These fears need to be challenged and they need to be conquered by all of us. Community artists are no different, and we are weighed down by our own lack of confidence and the lack of confidence in us that the established art world has. We can however overcome this by supporting each other, bringing in vision, creating opportunities for change, and by stepping into the full potential of our situation. I believe mutual assistance will enable us all to progress, indeed, it is the only way forward for the arts as a whole.

Community art needs to lead from the front rather than hide its light, and hope people will notice. There has always been a reluctance to lobby at any political and governmental levels by community artists, and I believe now is the time to start this.

Chapter Sixteen
Applied Creativity

Applied creativity for me, is the development of answers to social problems by 'applying' creativity. This does not necessarily mean the use of art, craft or any other visibly creative technique. Creativity is not just 'art' or 'craft', it is a way of thinking, a way of being. By applying creativity we can develop solutions to problems which are creative, imaginative and effective in the long term. I need to give some examples of applied creativity to indicate what I mean. To start on a simplistic level there is the placement of artists into unlikely situations, for instance 'artists in residence in prisons', what a simple but effective thing that can be. Good community artists will be enabling the inmates to develop their creativity, not just in terms of their painting, dance, or other skills, but in terms of their contribution to society. The stirring up of creativity and imagination can lead individuals to an understanding of who they are and what they need to do. This can mean they give up crime, they can change jobs, they can be inspired. The application of creativity will always lead to a wide range of outcomes, most of which are unexpected.

Applied creativity can also lead to the creation of posts where the artists are seen as equals to other professionals. That's something unique! Often the work we undertook in Germany was on an equal footing to the architect or engineer. It made such a change from the ways in which we were treated here in Britain. We were seen as influencers and of value to society as a whole.

Then we move into the more surreal realms of applying creativity, using simplicity, and seeing the 'bigger picture' being the linking factor. I heard of a scheme in America where the equivalent of Nursery Schools were recruiting men to work as 'teacher's aides' in the classes. The academic achievement levels of the boys were considerably lower than the girls, as we are now starting to have here. They identified the fact that these boys didn't have 'good male role models', as they were mostly from single family homes, or men being absent, or abusive, etc. The men who volunteered were to work as the lowest-of-the-lows in the schools, teachers aides, and the predominantly women teachers told them what to do. The men willingly obeyed the teachers in the classroom, and the children noticed what was happening. Over a five year period the academic achievement level of the boys started to increase, reaching parity with the girls, and there was a marked difference in their attitude to the teachers. What a wonderfully simple, effective example of applied creativity, increased academic achievement and it didn't cost anything. People looked at a problem and used their creativity to create a simple solution.

Another example is the improvements in mathematics and other areas of the curriculum in school children after being involved in large-scale arts projects. We all know it's true, but we haven't 'proved' it yet. It is unfortunately just about impossible to prove, but I know it happens, as do hundreds of teachers with whom we've worked.

There is an example in Scotland of a rehabilitation scheme for compulsive car thieves. The standard response to these young offenders is to put them in care, on probation, in prison, lock them away, and in doing so spend large amounts of money on them. This normally leads to them being taught other criminal skills, making further criminal contacts, and generally setting them up for a life long pursuit of petty and then serious crime. However, one authority is now putting these individuals through an intensive car maintenance and engineering programme. At the end of which many are now setting up legitimate businesses, and actually turning away from crime. A soft option? No, an option that benefits society, is cost effective, and looks at the 'bigger picture'.

These are all examples of imaginative thinking, creative engineering, they are all around us, applied creativity is happening all the time. We just don't recognise it as we have been taught to compartmentalise our experience. There are hundreds of small and large-scale schemes like these happening all over the world. We need to ensure that even more projects like these are started, even more imaginative schemes initiated and community artists are amongst those who can dare to think them into existence.

Teachers are amongst the most important people we have, they are teaching the next generation, they need to be our best people, not our dregs. For that reason I have always thought working in schools was hugely important. This does not mean that I am a frustrated teacher, but I support the teachers by offering a specialised experience, focused, led and informed by the creative process. Teachers need to be encouraged, supported and given the opportunity to try out new ideas. I have been employed as an artist working in schools and offer a different perspective, which the teachers wanted. I enable the students to do large-scale work, develop art skills, which teachers can't/won't do, due to the restrictions of the curriculum. Together we stimulate their imaginations, and show them the limitless nature of potential.

"To see education only as a preparation for something that happens later risks overlooking the needs and opportunities of the moment. Children do not hatch into adults after a secluded incubation at school. They are living their lives now. Helping them towards an independent and worthwhile life in the adult world of the future pre-supposes helping them to make sense of and deal with the experience and broaden children's experience through a broad and balanced curriculum. Literacy and numeracy are an important part of education. They should not be mistaken for the whole of it..." *xii

We need to see that what we are doing is very important, we are fulfilling a very vital role in society. It is a multi-layered and very complex activity.

The use of creativity has been effective in terms of making people happy for thousands of years, we love singing together, making arts and crafts, they cheer us up. Underneath that superficial view there lies a deeper and more significant meaning. The arts are mysterious, they allow us to work subconsciously and unconsciously, and they affect change. ***"The arts have a unique ability to break down barriers, encourage teamwork, discipline, responsibility and creative work amongst...people who might otherwise feel cut off from the rest of society." *xiii***

Creativity is a gateway into a better comprehension of our role in life. Often in community arts activities with groups, individuals have suddenly started to talk about their lives in an open and very honest way. It's as if the very act of getting their hands active (and dirty) somehow frees up their mind, and allows them to really 'see' who they are, and where they are going. As someone who has done this for over twenty years I know it is true, it has happened to me often enough. I can't 'prove' it. Increasingly however, there is an awareness of this not only in artists and creative people, but in local authorities, government agencies, even the European Union. Hundreds of community development projects are now underway throughout Britain and Europe, almost all of them have an arts element, almost all of them include creativity. This is fantastic progress which was unthinkable just twenty years ago.

I've lived in West Wales for over 5 years, I came with prejudices. As far as I was concerned all the good community artists lived and worked in South Wales, but my eyes have been opened. There are a huge amount of talented and caring artists, craftspeople, musicians, dancers, singers here, they just aren't as visible as the ones in South Wales. A lot of that has to do with their attitude to their own work and their worth. Many have given up the 'rat race', and have come for the quiet life. However, we all still need to make a living. There is a great deal of voluntary community art being undertaken, work in schools made by parents, work with community groups for free. This is all very wonderful, but it doesn't pay the bills, and a very common problem for these creative people is their inability to make ends meet through their given art skill. They tend to diversify, learn how to build, work in wood, do plumbing, whatever. In the end you actually have a very rounded and complete individual with a wide range of skills, but some are still frustrated by their lack of artistic opportunities. They feel they are not fulfilling their potential. This can be compounded by some of their attitudes towards the administration of projects, fund raising or any other 'office' activities. Many say to me *"That's the job of arts administrators",* and then bemoan the poor pay, conditions and projects which the few arts administrators or organisations in the area provide.

This is a common divide within modern creative people. They see their job as being the 'workshop', the activity, and then the funding, administration, running of the business, as something completely different. This is not true. The Pioneers were a classic example of taking art and administration as being equally important. We applied our creativity not only in workshops but in the ways in which we applied for, and received funding. Many of these creative people could actually be out there earning much more money, doing more exciting projects, if they had the confidence to apply for the funding themselves. It is essential that creative people re-claim their right to independent status. We are not medieval artisans at the beck and call of rich benefactors, we need to get serious. I do truly believe that there are a huge amount of jobs, employment and economic growth which can be stimulated by creative people. This will only come about if the creative people start the ball rolling, we can not expect those in power to suddenly turn on a tap, we have to show how good we are.

Creativity is not restricted to the time spent with a client group, creativity needs to be applied at all times. Apply creativity 24 hours a day, remember your dreams, they will show you how to be. There are many examples of artistic endeavour which has proven over large numbers of years how applied creativity can create employment and much more – Welfare State, Freeform, The Pioneers, Valley and Vale amongst others, and they all started as dreams or visions. There are so many examples of great work being generated by committed individuals as well, it is quite remarkable how much work there is out there!

Chapter Seventeen
It's a battleground out there

Really vibrant art can come directly from the community, it does not need the 'intervention' of professionals or enablers. This is something that happens very infrequently, but at least it happens sometimes. A project which was truly 'grassroots up' and actually based in a community, run by local people, was "Art In Action" in Bootle, Liverpool. It was a group of local people who set up a photography dark room in one of their homes, and the local children taught themselves how to use it. They toured and exhibited their work in many galleries and venues in Britain. They became a very highly politicised focus of the early 1980's, threatened with closure because the authorities thought the photographs were 'political'. In fact the local people and children were recording their lives, their motivations were never political, but the images they recorded could certainly been construed as such – desperate, grinding poverty is always political. It was a sad truth of the time (and any time) that anything which challenged the established view was seen as controversial and subversive. Children taking photographs of their homes and their friends became an attempt to bring down the government. In the end the project finished and the parents decided that enough was enough. The local authority had recently appointed a professional worker because the project was so successful, and this changed the participation by the children. Instead of them being in charge and leading, the 'professional' showed the way. At the time I was very sad to see it go, but as I look back I can see that the project had changed. It was also a brilliant example of knowing when to let go. Why hang on to something which is no longer as exciting or as 'good', move on, don't worry about it!

Such projects have a tendency to burn brightly for relatively short periods of time, they do not have to be sustained forever. Good work allows the people to continue at their own pace, and in the way in which they choose. Community art can thrive in the most unlikely of circumstances, so it is very difficult to predict how a project should be, or to adapt an existing model into a new community.

Most projects are however run by community artists, indeed, they were probably set up by them. A good community arts organisation changes and adapts to the wishes and needs of the people in it and for whom it works, it does not try to impose a system or a style. Most community arts groups are two or three people getting together and having a common goal. This is a very powerful thing, and can take many forms, shapes and directions. It is a combustible mixture, and can become very painful, there will be disagreements, falling outs and plenty of 'healthy discussion'. As Robert Hunter wrote ***"It embodied at times a religious fervor, at other times, a ruthlessness that bordered on savagery; it was borne out of desperation, out of fear, out of a love that transcended not only the boundaries of race and creed but even humanness. Corruption and greatness both played their parts and both took their tolls." *xiv*** He is describing the setting up of Greenpeace, and yet it is a common experience for so many community projects, collaboration is full of trials and tribulation.

This brings me onto a very important part of the process, change has to be an integral part of the organisation. Creative businesses have to be adaptable and flexible, often they are poorly paid and with long hours. To bring any stability and long term planning into such a structure is a very difficult task, and it can take many years. The Pioneers were a classic example of 'transmogrification' in the extreme – from being an exhibition space; to exhibiting in Galleries; to being stand up comedians; to being video artists; to being ‘scrap material workshoppers’; to being ‘artists in residence in schools’; to being ‘public artists’; to being employers; to being trainers; etc. If there is no change built into the structure then it will shrivel and die, however good the idea is now, in ten years people will be fed up with it!

Recently, we were visited by the very wonderful Hazel Kirkham who spent some time with us, and we talked through the whole concept of having run a business for twenty years. She explained how a great many businesses run in a very familiar pattern. Initially, they run on adrenaline, the twenty something enthusiasm brings about rapid development and change, the business becomes established, and creates a niche and market for the product. This then creates a plateau where you have really two choices, either you can continue trading in your niche and eventually retire, or you can create new markets and opportunities. Combining your new maturity with these opportunities, rather than reverting to your adrenal charged former way of working. Unfortunately, not many businesses, and especially businessmen, can see this. They become bored, their interest declines, and they never feel as though they have achieved as much as they could. Or alternatively they wreck everything and start over again, desperate for that adrenaline rush.

Change is happening at all times in any organisation and within you, whether you want it or not. You either have to adapt to it, or you will suddenly find that it isn’t as much fun as it was. As we are talking about creative businesses, that really should not be a problem. Unfortunately, there is a conformity within arts organisations, especially those receiving revenue funding from the Arts Council. Once they are successfully onto that gravy train, it is very difficult to get off. Some organisations were on the train very early and they now receive huge amounts of money, smaller more independent organisations receive a lot less, and therefore always stay about the same. Despite constant papers and discussion documents proclaiming that there will be change,the status quo has little changed in over twenty years. This is sad, because there is no real 'risk' money in the system. Young businesses need to be supported, but all too often they fall by the way side through exhaustion and fatigue, not really through their own fault.

I have been asked by a few organisations in Wales to assist in a range of projects looking at business creation, and the use of creativity within business as a whole. Amazingly, the skills I have learnt by juggling and being creative, are now starting to be recognised by people in mainstream business. Artists are being recognised as having expertise that is of value to the wider business world. This is a huge step, twenty years ago the concept of having an artist come in and teach you about business would have been laughed at so loudly as to make you hoarse. Nowadays, there are the first indications of interest from big business in terms of not only artists having business skills which are beneficial, but also that creativity can be applied in the work place. This has led to the development of business courses in 'creativity stimulation'. The use of dance, drama and other arts as 'bonding exercises', weekend courses in creativity. All of these things are expanding and their popularity is increasing. At the forefront of this movement are community artists, linking it all, and showing business how to get the best from their personnel. There is a long way to go, lots of people are still very disrespectful to the arts. Dismissing the creative process as superfluous and not of value to the community, but there is a tide turning, we need to be active participants in the expansion of these new areas of opportunity.

Chapter Eighteen
Training Needed Please

Creative people working together will often create larger, better, bigger and more effective work than when working alone. Collaborations can be very exciting, those that occur across art forms can be wonderful, collaborations which occur across continents can be truly inspiring. We are only beginning to see the potential of such work. The last hundred or so years have focused on individualism, elitism and intellectualisation in creativity. The next hundred will be much more about collaboration.

When we start working as a group it can often become quite fraught. A group is diverse. If everyone does the same as each other, it can get restrictive and claustrophobic. However, when there is a good range of people and skills, it gets interesting! Frequently groups are just two people, often that is enough. At times we had ten people and on occasions that felt too many and too much. Groups will change, the number of people comes and goes, often quite suddenly and without warning. My only advice is don't expect everyone to agree with you, flexibility and compromise are my middle names!

When we work as a team, or in a group, we have to become aware of other peoples' feelings and concerns. This is a good thing, it can increase your self-awareness and ability to communicate. It can bring into your consciousness issues which you have not addressed before. Often, group work, will enable you to see where your talents lie, and what you should allow others to, because they do them better. However, there is also a danger within a group of loosing your identity, loosing your own needs and strengths, which can be negative. It is all about balance, being honest about how you feel, and not becoming a martyr to any cause.

There are many artists led groups all over the UK, in Europe and USA. That is, they don't rely on administrators, or if they have one, the artists are still in control. More such initiatives need to be set up, more such projects need to be given time to mature. We shouldn't rely so heavily on administrative heavy organisations. Too often artist led initiatives have stumbled and fallen because no one was willing to take on the administrative responsibilities. Mainly this is due to the lack of good training and teaching of these skills on all arts related courses in Britain. The integration of administration skills into creativity, indeed the creative application of administrative skills is essential. Within the framework of artists collaborating there is actually a better chance of the administrative stuff getting done. Shared tasks don't seem so onerous and don't take so long. So, the jobs we all hate – accounts, applications, preparation and administration – are a lot easier when they are undertaken as a team rather than as individuals.

In the 1960's and 70's a lot of the political and arts activities were founded on a belief in the ability to bring about a 'revolution', and this was always talked about in terms of a mass movement. The new Millennium has brought a more reasonable understanding of what we need to do. For most of us it has brought about an understanding that we really can only ever change ourselves, the revolution is internal. In that sense we can only ever be responsible for ourselves, and the things we do. However, we do need to be aware of the consequences of all our actions, this is true responsibility. The consequences of working with a group of disenfranchised young people are huge, and at the same time we should not be intimidated by them. Our expectations of what we can reasonably achieve in a week or one day need to be fair, on ourselves, and those we work with.

Part of this process I feel is the development of work that is not owned by the artists, even though you are part of the process. If we can engender a sense of ownership, 'belonging' for the group which goes beyond passively participating, then we have achieved something worthwhile. The community artist must be prepared to step into the background and give the credit to others. In this sense the community artists are catalysts, they are a means to an end for the group they are working with. As a catalyst we may lead people to a better understanding of themselves, to a clearer view of certain relationships, we may even give them the idea that they can better themselves in terms of education or jobs. The role of a bridge is essential, but we are not dictating where they go, we are just giving them a view of what they are capable of.

Every five years or so the next generation of young artists 'discover' community art. New and different groups set up, people full of enthusiasm, they start working in music, dance, drama, whatever, and try to sustain themselves. All too often they are unable to sustain it, mainly because, like me, they are young whippersnappers who think they have discovered something new. They don't learn from the examples of others they plough on in their own lonely way. It's a familiar story, but we are collaborating more often now. There are now many community art groups and individuals out there, doing very good work and they are sharing their experiences.

"Beyond the role of the educationalist, sympathetic social worker or mere facilitator, community artists are emerging whose work can make a real, albeit localised contribution to the lives of people and communities as well as producing visually exciting, innovative and challenging artwork." *xv

This is what we need to keep in our minds, this is how we now need to see ourselves and to promote ourselves as such to as wide an audience as possible.

Part of this process is the understanding that community art is now creating a very good 'product'- be it music, dance, drama, or visual art. The products are actually very good art, very great art. Whilst community art was just a bit of therapy, just fun with children, it was not serious, now it has become a full grown art process and product, the excellence of the products speak for themselves.

A lot of artists and creative people want to be community artists. Those who want to become community artists need training. They will need to understand:-

* *how to collaborate, what is collaboration, what can you expect from other people – attitudinal concepts*
* *how to work with a range of clients – school children, adults, disadvantaged groups, etc.*
* *how to inspire and engender creativity amongst others*
* *how to move from one art skill to another*
* *how to be a catalyst for social change and what effects you can have on people*

Once they've learnt all of those things, they will then need to learn:-

* *how to administrate projects*
* *how to generate income for projects*
* *how to publicise and promote themselves*
* *how to plan in the long term*
* *how to evaluate projects*

In addition, there are large numbers of projects linked into community development and social inclusion work. Community artists are being integrated into the very fabric of social services, the infrastructure of our society. ***"Community Arts is about participation. It is about people defining and creating their own art and through this finding their own cultural voice... Those organisations presently demonstrating the best practice in community arts are***

those that have been established in partnership funding situations to provide a continuous provision of carefully nurtured and developed experiences." *xvi

This work is an on-going developmental process, not one-off workshops, and again the process and product needs to be appraised in the light of it's importance and it's ability to transform peoples lives. These are not prescriptive or patronising techniques, these are transformative experiences, which can lead to dramatic individual and cultural changes. As a recent graduate from an arts course you will need to learn and respect the history of this kind of work, so that you can then build upon what has gone before you. At present, it is very difficult to find out about the history of such work, and this aspect needs to be built into any new community arts courses as they are developed.

Chapter Nineteen
Participants in the future

In the early days of community art there was an arguement about where you worked. Roughly, community artists fell into two camps – those who worked specifically in one location, and those who would work anywhere. The theories at the beginning were pretty adventurous, I remember being told at a conference in the 1980's that one organisation held the view that:-

- *You had to work in only one community*
- *You had to not work in schools or institutions, but to work only with the really disenfranchised*
- *You had to 'Do yourself out of a job'*

This entailed working for so long in the community that the people you trained eventually took over your job as they learnt the skills and techniques. All very laudable but the end results still have to be proven, though many people who have come into community arts as participants are now practitioners.

This is a key issue. Anyone wanting to practice as a community artist needs to see the pitfalls and advantages of the two sides, and be aware of how this relates to their individual practice. If you only work in one community you have the opportunity to build fantastically strong connections; true community developments; true participation projects. You are however very prone to having your funding removed and being exposed financially. There can also be a tendency towards stagnation and inertia, which needs to be guarded against. If you go the other way, which The Pioneers did, you will be seen as 'cowboys'; being 'parachuted in'; as 'outsiders'. There is also no sense of stability leading to a tendency to burn out, stress and skimming participation. It is not easily resolved, and it certainly needs to be constantly reviewed. I think, nowadays, there are a greater diversity of opportunities available, and it is not such a clear cut decision in terms of working one way or the other. As a community artist you can now combine the two ways of working.

"We define community arts as collaboration with people within group settings to produce work which communicates their feelings and ideas. The process and the work produced may be celebratory, reflective or campaigning, the aim of which is to develop an enhanced sense of place or community. The products of the work are jointly owned by all those who have collaborated in their creation. Community arts workers are professionals who offer to the public a range of artistic and media skills to realise their potential to create meanings rather than simply to receive entertainment."*xvii To define the arts as being such a process is to start to see how we have all been sold short over the past 30 if not 200 years. We couldn't have defined it that way in 1970, we have become something which was not even envisioned in those days.

In terms of the participants in the work, I want to look at what we can reasonably expect their experience to be. At a very basic level the participants need to be in a friendly environment, be happy and be learning. It is the artists' responsibility to ensure that this happens every time. In addition I believe unconsciously or consciously the participants need to be challenged, particularly in their assumptions about art and creativity. I tend to work with people who have never met 'an artist' before, and for many of them they come with a lot of prejudices. Even the small children giggle and guffaw when I state: *"I am an artist".* So, one of my jobs is to ensure that they understand how being an artist is OK. To understand that artists are useful, worthy and something to aspire to, this is quite a step for a lot of people in Britain. For them to understand that I am an ordinary person with a wife, two teenage children, a mortgage, and employing four people in an arts business as well, is asking a lot. If they understand this and have a good time making some mosaics or whatever, I've worked hard and well. I know this may seem irrelevant, but it isn't, it is very important. The significance of ordinary people thinking and knowing to be an artist is a good thing should not be overlooked. If enough people think it then a sea change of perception will come about.

I have been able to employ myself and other people to 'do art' for over twenty years. Before I and many others did this, most *artists*, let alone ordinary people, thought that it was impossible. In the 1960's no one thought you could make a living as a DJ, most footballers earned very little money. Times change. If community art is going to grow and flourish it needs to be perceived as a career path, not only by artists, but by the general public. My responsibility to the next generation of creative people is to ensure that they have a real chance of gaining worthwhile employment. So, in order to overturn conservative thought patterns, we must truly democratise our practice and increase opportunity. When we work with children, we nurture the future - a future community who accept participating in the arts as a right - not as an 'add on'. Anyway, you never know who that 8 year old will become – a planner, architect, future Culture Minister!

In addition to the participants gaining an understanding of what it is to be an artist, there are side effects from this work which are peculiar to me. I am a man and as such a rare animal in Primary Schools on the high-risk estates on which we work. The young people I work with do not have many good male role models in terms of behaviour towards women, children or life in general. My being there, as a man who is employed as an artist, who treats women and children with respect, who plays with them, and who gives them encouragement and praise, is very important. Do not underestimate the change in later life that this type of role modeling can bring about. This effect can be in the detail, as ever. Young men see me as being the boss, they see me as being in charge, and they watch what I do. One of the things I do is to make sure that all jobs are shared, so I clean up after everyone. Many boys remark on this, *"That's a job for the cleaning lady".* We need to be aware of the impact of everything we do, that way we are effective and good community artists.

Obviously, I would also expect the participants to gain other things from a project. These are very difficult to define, but we need to try to ennumerate them in one form or another. Mostly they are personal and unarticulated, and there lies our struggle to evaluate them or show how they have been affected. The challenge for community art in the future is to *prove* what we know to be true. Nowadays the appraisal of community art has become a very important issue. As can be seen from the diversity of examples in this slim volume a great deal of issues could be appraised and accredited, but the actual setting up of structures and frameworks which work and show value is still very difficult.

Initially, the number of people participating in a project was used as a marker -hundreds of children taking part equated to good project- it isn't that simple. Recently I worked in three schools in Llanelli, at the first they gave us a pair of autistic twins who had never worked alongside mainstream pupils before, we successfully integrated them. At the second, we were able to build sufficient trust that one child talked about how her brothers were murdered, which the school didn't know! At the third, I worked with an elective mute, who spoke to us for the first time. I would never have put those as the criteria for the work at it's outset, you just never know!

Art is a very mysterious experience. When we create art we participate in an unconscious and mysterious practice. Mystery does not lend itself to appraisal, spontaneity can not be put on a tick list. The difference between a good project and a bad one can be in an attitude, a vulnerability, or in deviating from the original brief.

I believe that somewhere in the work being presently undertaken in Britain we have the starting blocks for a solid appraisal system. I have never seen my job as being one allied to appraisal and such issues. Thus far I have just 'done it'. I know that is not enough, but I don't have the expertise or knowledge presently to take it further. In the end, all I can do is say what has happened and trust it will be used by others in the future. How the next generation of artists and creative people develop this is up to them, I've done my bit, and all I can do is look to the future.

After over twenty odd years, I have now 'retired' (joke). I have become self-employed, a consultant, no longer working frantically to employ five people, and I must say it has probably saved my sanity! By easing off I have been able to do some things which I haven't for a long time - think, look back, and even started to paint for myself. This book is a result of easing off, being able to re-assess who I am and what I do. Interestingly, I am now almost exclusively employed outside the arts, I very rarely make mosaics. I am employed to teach teachers, community and youth workers, work with spirituality and ritual, working mainly with teenage boys and men. I am able to stretch myself and the horizons of the work I do, and this is very gratifying. Creativity and collaboration are powerful tools for change and when applied with love and trust, faith in the process, they will always stretch and expand. Creativity and collaboration are primal instincts deep within our souls, they have been suppressed in the current culture.

Step back into creative collaboration and you can not fail to be moved, to be enlightened, and set free. Through having experienced so much creativity and collaboration, I am able to apply myself to a wide range of situations, confident that I can help. At present, I am working with fathers from the probationary service, enabling them to understand their role and responsibilities. I am able to work with people to create ceremonies and rituals to honour themselves and their ancestors. I am advising a wide range of local community based initiatives to create jobs and employment for people.

When I first started out I accepted every job I was offered, I ran as fast as I could just to establish myself, and support the concepts I believed in. I have matured with experience, age, and the inevitable need to slacken off the pace. In the 1990's I first started to come across third generational unemployed people, and we tried to help them gain employment. Nowadays, I am working with fourth generation teenagers, and the really sad factor in their lives, is their lack of imagination. They can't see their way out of their family and social situations. They have never been shown how to play, they have such a lack of vision or hope for the future, it makes me very sad. This is why it is so important that creative people, people with hope, imagination and spirit, continue to do this work. We are beacons of light and beauty, and we can affect changes however small in other people's lives.

Notes

*i **Su Braden** "Artists and People" Routledge and Kegan Paul 1978
*ii **Gillo Dorfles** in "Art Today" by Edward Lucie-Smith Phaidon 1983
*iii **Jared Diamond** "The Rise and Fall of the Third Chimpanzee" Radius 1991
*iv and v **P. Kropotkin** "Mutual Aid A Factor of Evolution" William Heinemann 1902
*vi **Mike Ormsby** "Call Yourselves Artists" The Pioneers Ltd 1985
*vii **Richard Cork** "Art For Whom" An Exhibition Serpentine Gallery, London May 1978
*viii **Konrad Lorenz** "The Waning of Humaneness" Unwin Hyman 1988
*ix **Margaret Morgan** "ART 4-11 Art in the early years of schooling" Blackwell Education 1988
*x "Arts and communities" produced by the **Community Development Foundation** 1992
*xi **Malcolm Dickson** "Art With People" AN Publications 1995
*xii "The Arts In Schools" **Calouste Gulbenkian Foundation** 1982
*xiii "Sport, The Arts and Social Exclusion" **Department of Culture, Media and Sport**. July 1999
*xiv **Robert Hunter** "The Greenpeace Chronicle" Picador 1979
*xv **Emma Safe** "Young Community Artist (YCA)" Artists Newsletter January 2001
*xvi **National Arts and Media Strategy**, Proposal for Community Arts, June 1992
*xvii **The Forum for Community Arts in South East Wales** "A Shock To The System" 1988

Bibliography

Aurobindo, Sri *"The Mother Questions and Answers"* Ashram Trust 1973

Braden , Sue *"Artists and People"* Routledge and Kegan Paul 1978

Byron, Robert *"First Russia, Then Tibet"* London: Macmillan and Co. 1933

Calouste Gulbenkian Foundation *"The Arts In Schools"* 1982

Cameron, Julia *"The Artists' Way"*, London: Pan Books 1994

Carson, Rachel *"Silent Spring"* Houghton Mifflin 1962

Clements, Harry *"Alfred Russel Wallace "* London: Hutchinson and Co 1983

Cork, Richard *"Art For Whom" An Exhibition* Serpentine Gallery, London May 1978

Community Development Foundation *"Arts and communities"* 1992

Darwin, Charles *"On the Origin of Species..."* London: John Murray 1859

Department of Culture, Media and Sport *"Sport, The Arts and Social Exclusion"* July 1999

Diamond, Jared *"The Rise and Fall of the Third Chimpanzee"* London: Radius 1991

Dickson, Malcolm *"Art With People"* AN Publications 1995

Forum for Community Arts in South East Wales *"A Shock To The System"* 1988

Fox, John *"Eyes on Stalks"* London: Methuen 2002

Hawking, Stephen *"A Brief History of Time"* Bantam 1998

Hughes, Robert *"Nothing If Not Critical"* Harvill Panther 1990

Hunter, Robert *"The Greenpeace Chronicle"* London: Pan Books 1979

Kelly, Owen *"Storming the Citadels"* London:Comedia 1984

Kropotkin, Peter *"Mutual Aid A Factor of Evolution"* London: William Heinemann 1902

"Modern Science and Anarchism" London: Freedom Press 1912

de Leon, Juana Ponce *"Our Word Is Our Weapon"* Serpent's Tail 2001
Lorenz, Konrad *"The Waning of Humaneness"* London: Unwin 1988
Lucie-Smith , Edward *"Art Today"* Phaidon 1983
Matarasso,Francois *"Use or Ornament? The Social Impact of Participation in the Arts"* Comedia 1997
Morgan,Margaret *"ART 4-11 Art in the early years of schooling"* Blackwell Education 1988
National Arts and Media Strategy, *Proposal for Community Arts,* June 1992
Neill, A.S. *"Summerhill School, A New View of Childhood",* New York: St. Martin's Press 2002
Ormsby, Mike *"Call Yourselves Artists"* The Pioneers Ltd 1985
Prechtel, Martîn *"Secrets of the Talking Jaguar"* London: Element 1998
Joseph Rowntree Foundation *"Creative Regeneration"* 2001 *"Arts and Regeneration"* 2000 www.jrf.org.uk
Russell, Stephen *"Barefoot Doctor's Handbook for the Urban Warrior"* London: Piatkus 1998
Schwarz, Walter and Dorothy *"Breaking Through"* Cornwall: Green Books 1987
South West Arts *"Turning Points"* 2001, www.swa.co.uk
Voluntary Arts Wales *"Worth Making a Song and Dance About"* 2002 www.vaw.org.uk
Wallace, Alfred Russel *"Studies Scientific and Social"* London: Macmillan and Co 1900
Weiss, P. A. *"Hierarchically Organized Systems in Theory and Practice"* New York: Hafner 1971

Page 29 to 30

The example of the Harp Industry comes from conversations with Allan Shiers

Page 57 to 61

Taken from an article I wrote for "Mailout" magazine in 2002

Further Information And Resources List

MAGAZINES/WEB SITES

Arts Industry:
01986 834250 www.artsindustry.co.uk
Arts Professional:
01954 250600 www.artsprofessional.org.uk
Interchanges: (Centre for Creative Communities):
020 7247 5385 www.creativecommunities.org.uk
Mailout Magazine:
01246 207070 www.e-mailout.org
Ninety Five Percent (Youth Arts network):
01379 644200 nick.nra@virgin.net
Sounding Board (Sound Sense):
01449 736287 www.soundsense.org

OTHER SOURCES OF INFORMATION

Arts Council of England
http://www.artscouncil.org.uk

Arts Council of Northern Ireland
http://www.artscouncil-ni.org

Arts Council of Scotland
http:// www.sac.org.uk

Arts Council of Wales
http://www.ccc-acw.org.uk

Ashden Directory of Environment and Drama
http://www.ashdendirectory.org.uk
British Arts Festivals Association
http://www. artsfestivals.co.uk
British Council - http://www.britishcouncil.org
Calouste Gulbenkian Foundation
http://www.gulbenkian.org.uk
Centre for Creative Communities
http://www.creativecommunities.org.uk
Creative Exchange
http://www.creativexchange.org
Euclid - http://www.euclid.co.uk
International Intelligence on Culture
http://www.intelculture.org
National Association of Youth Theatres
http://www.nayt.org.uk
National Endowment for Science, Technology and the Arts
http://www.nesta.org.uk
Visiting Arts - http://www.britcoun.org/visitingarts
Voluntary Arts Network
http://www.voluntaryarts.org
Wales Association of Community - Artists group
A_C_A@yahoogroups.com
Wales Council for Voluntary Action
www.wcva.org.uk

Soundoftheheart accept no responsibility for any inaccuracies in the above information.

PIONEERS
IMPROVING YOUR SCHOOL ENVIRONMENT
By Nick Clements and Sarah Osborne

This book will inspire parents and teachers to think about ways of improving the educational experience of the children in schools. The expertise which The Pioneers have gained applies to nursery, primary and secondary schools. This publication explains in simple stages how you can plan and develop your improvement strategy and it is illustrated by examples of work made by schools in South Wales, an area well known for its community spirit, but severely lacking in financial support systems. Yet despite these restrictions The Pioneers have worked with over 35,000 children and raised in excess of £5 million towards the work.

Published by
NSEAD
The Gatehouse,
Corsham Court,
Corsham,
Wiltshire SN13 0BZ
ISBN 0-904684-17-2

THE PIONEERS
MURALS, MOSAICS, MADNESS AND MYTHS
By Nick Clements

This full colour book deals with the adventures and stories behind the artists-led group called The Pioneers. Set up in 1981 and closed in 2004, they became legendary figures in the world of community art. This publication is the funny and sad tale of their fortunes and misfortunes. It tells the amazing stories of the initial days of community art on the hoof, travelling from community to community in Wales. Through to working in schools accompanied by the diversification of skills, and finally the development of professionalism, eventually the creation of full time employment for artists.

It is a beautiful document, illustrated with over 40 photographs of the large scale art works they produced, not only in Wales, but throughout Europe and beyond. These will inspire artists, teachers and those interested in bringing creativity into the community. It makes an argument for the continuation of radical and adventurous art, hoping to encourage artists to collaborate and work in a variety of mediums and with a wide range of people.

Published by
Sound of the Heart
Cilgraig
Capel Dewi
Llandysul
Ceredigion SA44 4PP
ISBN 0-9547302-0-8